Teaching in the Key of Life

a collection of the writings of

Mimi Brodsky Chenfeld

A 1992–93 NAEYC Comprehensive Membership benefit

National Association for the Education of Young Children, Washington, DC

National Association for the Education of Young Children

1509 16th Street N.W.
Washington, DC 20036-1426
202-232-8777 or 1-800-424-2460

The National Association for the Education of Young Children (NAEYC) attempts through its publications program to provide a forum for discussion of major issues and ideas in our field. We hope to provoke thought and promote professional growth. The view expressed or implied are not necessarily those of the Association. NAEYC wishes to thank the author, who made available to us her many essays from which this collection was drawn.

Library of Congress Catalog Card Number: 93-085701
ISBN Catalog Number: 0-935989-57-9
NAEYC #315

Editor: Carol Copple
Copyeditor: Millie Riley
Design: Jack Zibulsky
Production: Betty Nylund Barr
Editorial assistance: Penny Atkins

Printed in the United States of America

Photo credits: p. iv Top—© Allen Zak; Bottom left—© Allen Zak; Bottom right—© Judy Panek. p. v Top left—© Judy Panek; Top right—© Larry Hamill; Bottom left—© Larry Hamill; Bottom right—© *Columbus Dispatch.*

Previously published essays: NAEYC gratefully acknowledges the following copyright holders for their permission to reprint Mimi Chenfeld's originally published writings (a few under other titles), re-edited for this book.

pp. xii–xiii from *Language Arts,* © Copyright 1985 (December) by the National Council of Teachers of English.

pp. 4–6 from *Educational Leadership,* © Copyright 1992 (February) by the Association for Supervision and Curriculum Development.

pp. 7–8 from *Phi Delta Kappan,* © Copyright 1991 (December) by Phi Delta Kappa, Inc.

pp. 11–12 from *Educational Leadership,* © Copyright 1989 (November) by the Association for Supervision and Curriculum Development.

pp. 13–15 (appeared as "I'm Worried About Our Kids) from *Day Care and Early Education,* © Copyright 1984 (Fall) by Human Sciences Press, Inc.

pp. 18–20 from *Young Children,* © Copyright 1991 (September) by NAEYC.

pp. 21–26 from *Phi Delta Kappan,* © Copyright 1976 (November) by Phi Delta Kappa, Inc.

pp. 31–34 from *Young Children,* © Copyright 1990 (November) by NAEYC.

pp. 35–39 from *Scholastic Teacher,* © Copyright 1973 (January) by Scholastic, Inc.

pp. 42–45 from *Language Arts,* © Copyright 1987 (November) the National Council of Teachers of English.

pp. 46–49 (appeared as "A Letter to Ms. Byrne") from *Educational Leadership,* © Copyright 1991 (May) by the Association for Supervision and Curriculum Development.

pp. 50–53 from *Day Care and Early Education,* © Copyright 1990 (Summer) by Human Sciences Press, Inc.

pp. 54–55 from *Young Children,* © Copyright 1993 (September) by NAEYC.

pp. 58–63 from *Young Children,* © Copyright 1987 (March) by NAEYC.

pp. 64–68 from *Language Arts,* © Copyright 1989 (April) by the National Council of Teachers of English.

pp. 69–71 (appeared as "From Catatonic to Hyperactive: Randy Snapped Today") from *Young Children,* © Copyright 1989 (May) by NAEYC.

pp. 72–74 (appeared as "Words of Praise: Honey on the Page") from *Language Arts,* © Copyright 1985 (March) by the National Council of Teachers of English.

pp. 75–77 (appeared as "Newsletter From the Field") from *Momentum,* © Copyright 1993 by the National Catholic Educational Association.

Previously unpublished essays:

pp. 9–10 and 27–30. © Copyright 1993 by NAEYC.

About the Author

Once, when Mimi Chenfeld happened to be visiting a school in Worthington, Ohio, on "kindergarten assessment day," she was handed an application form by a volunteer mistaking her for a prospective kindergartner's parent. Having found the school abuzz with active learning and lively goings-on— right down to a flamingo motif in the restroom–Mimi filled out the form like this:

Child's Name: *Mimi Brodsky Chenfeld*

Child's Date of Birth: *30 March 1935*

What Else Would You Like To Tell Us About the Child?

She would rather stand than walk, walk than stand, dance than walk. Even though she is a little immature, she would love to go to kindergarten in a school with flamingos in the bathroom and love in the classroom.

Mimi Brodsky Chenfeld, M.Ed., is a teacher, writer, and national consultant. She is the author of *Teaching Language Arts Creatively (2nd edition)* and *Creative Experiences for Young Children (2nd edition upcoming)*, published by Harcourt Brace, as well as numerous stories, poems, essays, and books. Her infectious joy in teaching, lively writing, and wisdom about what engages children have made her a popular contributor to *Young Children* and other publications for educators and parents.

Born in New York City, Mimi Chenfeld has lived in Columbus, Ohio, since 1970. She began her teaching career in 1956. Presently, she is an artist-educator in the Artists in the Schools program and on the staff of the Early Childhood Department of the Leo Yassenoff Jewish Center in Columbus. She leads the international folk dance program of Ohio State University's Hillel Foundation and the Johnson Park Middle School performing folk dance group, The Footsteps.

Mimi travels extensively, lecturing and conducting workshops, seminars, and training with classroom teachers, parents, university students and others—all under the umbrella of "teaching in the key of life." One kindergartner summed up the author best when she said: "That Mimi is a very playful girl!"

To Len, and Callie Rose, and to all the kids and everyone who loves them.

Contents

Amanea 300x

FI + 495

10.8.9

Mrs. Chenfield

Feet⇒

The children's art and letters that appear throughout this volume come from the many, many thank-yous that Mimi Chenfeld has received over her 30 plus years of sharing time with children in their classrooms. In most cases we do not have sufficient identifying information about the children to acknowledge them by name and age. Instead, we wish to thank them collectively for their eloquent expressions of what they have loved and learned in their time with Mimi.

Dear Mrs. Chenfield
    I really liked the dances we did. And I think your nice. Reimber when you said use brain power I used my brain power and it worked.

                                                    Sincerly,
                                                    Kiesha

Foreword

When learning a new swimming stroke, would you like to be told how to do it? Or would you rather have someone *show* you how it looks and give *you* the chance to try it out yourself? It's like that for teaching, too. Participating in exciting classroom happenings is far more powerful than reading a list of how-tos.

Mimi Brodsky Chenfeld knows this very well. Much of the time she can be found in classrooms and workshops, helping to make exciting things happen. The teachers, administrators, parents, and children who get to join Mimi in person are especially lucky. But, we all are fortunate because she is also gifted at bringing these exciting classroom happenings to the printed page. In her writing, as in the classroom, Mimi doesn't *tell* us how to teach. She pulls us right in.

What Mimi does is *not* to demonstrate a particular method for teachers to copy—monkey see, monkey do. Rather, she shares her passionate convictions about teaching in "the key of life"—which can take many forms, but always means that one's heart and mind are fully engaged with the hearts and minds of the children. Mimi shows us snapshots—"home videos" may be more like it—of her own teaching and of dozens of wonderful teachers she's seen in action. And she challenges each reader to find his or her own unique ways to teach in the key of life.

Mimi Chenfeld has always been a firm believer in the maxim, "nothing without joy," that underlies the early childhood program in Reggio Emilia, Italy. At a time when so many American educators are intensely interested in what they can learn from Reggio Emilia, we are particularly pleased to be publishing Mimi Chenfeld's collected work; every page pulses with joy, wonder, and the celebration of learning. Like the *pedagogistas* of Reggio, she knows the value of movement, visual arts, and other means of expression in the child's life and learning. As these essays show, Mimi has also long espoused another theme shared by Reggio Emilia and the best of U.S. educational programs: The teacher is a co-learner along with the children. Mimi always conveys her respect for children's learning instincts and capacities—she takes her cues from them. And she expects children, whatever their age, to participate fully in directing their own learning.

Creating this collection

Since Mimi Chenfeld has been teaching for more than 36 years and writing about teaching for nearly as long, choosing a couple dozen pieces for this collection was not easy. Nor was it simple to group them into sections. Why? Watch Mimi in the classroom! I dare you to tell me where her teaching of language arts leaves off and her movement program (or any other subject) begins. Visual arts, music, language, science, math, social studies—they intermingle seamlessly, a rich and dynamic whole.

Similarly, Mimi's writings cannot be pigeonholed into neat chapters. Although we divide this collection into four sections, any one of the essays fits comfortably in any section. The four sections are as follows:

• *Teaching in the Key of Life*

These essays introduce Mimi's favorite themes and give us visions of classrooms bursting at the seams with learning and celebration.

• *Valuing the Real FUNdamentals*

Playfulness, humor, joy, and the love of learning are the real "basics" that should abound in any environment where children spend their time.

• *Tuning in to Children*

Children will teach us how to reach them if we tune in to what delights them, intrigues them, makes them laugh. What we need to learn above all, Mimi shows us, is to "hang out" with children.

• *Teaching From the Heart*

At the core of all education that makes a difference in children's lives—beneath all the methods, materials, and curricula—is a teacher who cares about each child, who teaches from the heart.

The children's letters and art that you see throughout the book were gleaned from the thousands of "thank-yous" received by Mimi over the years. They speak volumes about what children value, not just in Mimi Brodsky Chenfeld, but in all those who teach in "the key of life."

—*Carol Copple*

Teach Me in the Key of Life

I am waiting for you.

I have been waiting all my life

to spend this time

with you.

*   *   *

I am full of questions, adventures, wonder, curiosity,
imagination.

I am full of fears, doubts, confusions, nightmares, dreams.

I am the Cowardly Lion. I need a badge for courage.
So do you.

I am the Tin Man. So tight. I forgot about my heart.
How's your heart?

I am the Scarecrow. Hangin' so loose my brain feels
unhinged. Does yours?

Sometimes I'm

GrumpySleepyDopeyBashfulDocSneezyHappy.

Sometimes I'm seven new dwarfs as yet unnamed.

*   *   *

I love to sing.

I know the words to 2,437 songs.

Teach me through songs.

Let me paint, doodle, scribble, draw, carve, fix,
sketch–DO.

I can't keep still.

I'm a spaced-out, far-out, Star Wars, Superman IV,
rock 'n' roll, disco,

punk, psychedelic, tuned-out, right-on, cool age,
electronic, stereo,

video games, computerized, technicolor, ten-
speed kid!

I need action!

Keep it moving!

* * *

I love to read baseball cards, album covers, TV
    schedules, movie ads,

license plates, T-shirts, buttons, posters, cartoons,
    cereal boxes,

recipes, highway signs, historical markers, magazines,
    picture books,

sad stories, weird poems, animal histories, lost-and-
    found boards. . . .

* * *

Let me ask my questions— even if you don't know the
    answers.

Dumb questions, like who started numbers?

Do caterpillars know they're going to turn into
    butterflies?

Where does the white go when the snow melts?

Why does time fly?

How do we see?

What do you see?

_____

**(Special thanks to Stevie Wonder, who named his
album Songs in The Key of Life)**

* * *

It's not my birthday, but every day can't we celebrate
SOMETHING?

Colors, seasons, Tuesdays, Mexico, circles, houses,
    maps, our names, numbers, one seed, our journals,
    favorite books, inventions, rivers, peace!

Can we celebrate our country on the fourth of October
    or the twelfth of May?

We don't have school on the fourth of July!

Every day let's celebrate SOMETHING!

Life—the wonder and power and miracle of Life—of
    being here, learning together, with all our
    fantastic powers.

* * *

Surprise me. Amaze me. Startle me. Challenge me.
    Try me. Laugh with me.

Love me. Teach me

in "the key of life,"

and I promise I'll

surprise, amaze, startle, challenge, try, enjoy,

and love YOU!

I.

Teaching

in the

Key of Life

Teaching in the key of life can take many forms, but it always means that one's heart and mind are fully engaged with the hearts and minds of children.

Avalon school!

To day miss mimi came to avalon.
She was nise to us
we hade fun
we learned to do a indien dance.
It was so fun that I got it sided I ran out side and play.
  She tot us hoe to do a egel dance.

Jason

3

Whatever else good teaching is, it is teaching in which our hearts and minds are fully engaged in connecting with children's hearts and minds. This is what Mimi Chenfeld calls teaching in the key of life.

Teaching
in the
Key of Life

During the lunch break at a recent conference of early childhood educators—all miraculously keeping their spirits high despite low salaries, benefits, and prestige—a parent came in and addressed the group.

"Everyone who ever loved my children and gave them wonderful experiences is in this room. That's why I came—to tell them how much I appreciate them. Now, my kids are scattered throughout the grades and, let me tell you, they dearly miss these people."

While these words are gratifying, I, like that parent, am distressed about what happens to too many children beginning in their elementary years.

We have the best research reminding us of healthy, happy, positive, holistic, active, interactive, playful, multifaceted ways children learn *best*. Despite this wealth of knowledge plus the even more powerful information from our own hearts, why are so many children still *learning* that *learning* is a grim, scary, closed-in, super-structured, silent process where failure, humiliation, alienation, and disappointment are present every day?

Once children learn such lessons, it is hard— often impossible—to reach them, to welcome them back, to remind them of their worth, to hallow their gifts. They are lost to us. They don't drop out. They *fall* out!

Why is play downplayed? Let's call play "work" and get on with it. Why are there so many thorns in so many kindergartens—the "gardens of children"?

Why should a boy who loves blocks better than any toys in the whole, wide world run excitedly to his first day of kindergarten, only to return at the end of that momentous day with slumped shoulders and teary eyes and angrily announce, "Mommy, there are no blocks in kindergarten! Mommy, you lied! You said it would be fun!"

I think there are new kinds of blocks in lots of kindergartens!

* * *

Why are some first graders—active, energetic, verbal, and curious— carrying dittos home by the package? One child was out of school with the flu. Each day his sister carried his homework to him. His dad showed me the collection of almost 30 dittos. When the boy recovered, he begged his parents NOT to send him back to school. In schools that teach in "the key of life," sick children get healthy. In schools that teach in "the key of death," healthy children get sick. Every time we use paper, we should remember that trees sacrificed their lives. When trees know they will be turned into nothing but dittos, they become weeping willows.

A tree wept for the kindergarten boy whose colors didn't stay in the dark lines outlined by his teacher. He added a few lines of his own. When he asked his teacher if she liked his picture, she didn't need to tell him. Her expression showed her disapproval; but in case there was any doubt of her feelings, she added, "I think you can do a lot better." The boy's face fell. After dragging around home for almost a week, he finally told his mom that he was a terrible artist, hated coloring, and didn't want to go back to school.

His mom's conference with his teacher was rocky. "Don't baby him," the teacher warned. "These children need to know it's a harsh world. When children ask me something, I tell the truth. What would you have me do?"

The teacher could have considered these suggestions for alternative responses to a child's question, "Do you like my picture?"

1. "The important question is—How do *you* like the picture?"

2. "Let's look at your picture. Tell me about it."

3. "I see you especially like green—that cloud you drew looks to me like a little puff of cotton. How does it look to you?"

Probably, a child named Vincent asked his teacher how she liked his drawing of a starry night, and she said, "I think you can do a lot better, Vincent. These stars are entirely too swirly." And so, Vincent dragged himself home and cut off his ear. (Now you know the real story!)

* * *

A first grade teacher told me about this incident. One day, early in the school year, at 11:30 in the morning, a child went to the closet, took his jacket and bag, and started for the door. Stopping him, the teacher gently asked him where he was going. "Home," he said. "Honey," she told him, "You don't go home yet. You're in first grade now. You get to stay all day." Placing his hands on his hips, and with eyes wide, the boy asked, "Well, who the hell signed me up for this?"

I found one day a message left on my answering machine by Barbara Selinger who teaches in the key of life in New Jersey. She told about the first grader who raced home after school and sent this alarming announcement throughout the house: "Mommy! We have a SPELLING TEST tomorrow! Mommy! Don't they know I'm only six? I'm too young to have a SPELLING TEST!"

I hope we're not too *old* to get the message!

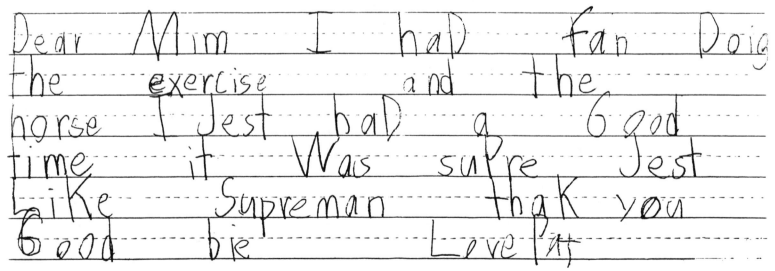

Dear Mim I had fan Doig the exercise and the horse I Jest had a good time it Was supre Jest Like Supreman thaK you Good bie Love Pat

Four simple strategies will help anyone who works with children move toward more creative teaching.

In Four Easy Nudges— Everything You Need To Know About Being a Creative Teacher

One week before I'm scheduled to present a staff development/in-service training program on creative teaching— or, as I subtitle all my offerings, "Teaching in the Key of Life"— the telephone rings. On the line is the principal of the school where I'm scheduled to appear.

"Now, Mimi. We have some 'linears' here, some 'concretes'! They aren't going to be happy with your whirly, circular, random presentation. They want strategies! They want techniques! They want a list! They want numbers! Can you give them some numbers?"

Being a flexible, circular type who truly wants to please, I work out some strategies. As a believer in the old hymn "'Tis a Gift To Be Simple," I keep my list simple—just four items (none of which will succeed as techniques unless practiced in an environment of trust, safety, and respect; for when students are afraid to ask, to share, to fail, no strategies for creative teaching will work). I call these, "four easy nudges."

To keep my fellow, circular thinkers happy, I remind them that these four easy nudges for creative teaching can be rearranged in any order. Got a pencil? Here they are:

1. *What else?* Merely asking this question will trigger the response: "More, more, more!" What else can we find out about the early settlers? What else can you share about your pet gerbil? What else can we think of for our spring program? What else do we want to know about the Beatles? "What else?" is not smug. It helps us to expand our horizons and reminds us that we can never completely finish a subject or an idea. There is always more to discover, to learn, to ask, to wonder about. "What else?" keeps our minds open.

2. *What if?* Merely asking this question will automatically trigger the imagination. What if the wolf in "Little Red Riding Hood" had been rehabilitated and reformed? What if we could translate the songs of whales into English? What if we had experienced the great journey westward? What if this house were really haunted? What if we began a story with its ending? What if the founding fathers had sung the Constitution?

3. *Show it!* This nudge invites us into the world of enriched, exciting, multilevel learning experiences. Take an idea or concept, or book, or poem, or fact! Showing gives validity to different ways of learning and comprehending. Show an idea— demonstrate it in words, in pictures, in music, in dance, in sculpture, in graphs, in reports, in an interview, in a discussion, with a puppet, on a bulletin board, as a newspaper, in clay, in a play, in any way that communicates.

4. *Fake it!* Children used to teachers and parents who want the right answer may need this nudge to give them permission to try something new or different. Take a stab at it! Make believe you can do it! Don't worry! Hang loose! Stay cool! If you can't do something perfectly, it's OK to try anyway. "Fake it" invites participation and encourages involvement. It draws a circle that encompasses everyone. No one is ever left out.

* * *

Well, that covers it! When should you begin? How about right now? Do I have any last-minute advice? Have fun! and, if you're unsure, fake it!

In the tumultuous crosscurrents that batter teachers and children today, holding on to strong metaphors of what the classroom can be for children—lifeboat, treasure ship, Allie-Allie-in-Free, and more—can help us keep our bearings.

Room 4 on the Second Floor

This is an easy time to be in education. . . . Not!!!

Many of us are caught in the educational turmoil, with daily blaring headlines criticizing, demeaning, demanding. Statistics, polls, and surveys contribute to the snarl of shifting definitions and changing educational expectations. How can teachers respond to the tumultuous pressures and conflicting messages? How can we find ways to keep our sanity, our humor, our sense of wonder?

The powerful magic of language can help to keep us sane. Let a metaphor into your life. Better yet, let a mix of metaphors into your life.

My room is Room 4 on the Second Floor. It's more than a room, it's a city of refuge. It's the eye in the storm's center—that calm, still place in the midst of the swirling, tangling winds. My room is more than a room, it's Allie-Allie-in-Free. You can't get tagged out, it's home plate. It's a lifeboat. It's the underground railroad.

In Room 4 on the Second Floor, I am Charlotte. With my children I spin a special safety net of a web. In it we weave life-affirming, life-saving words. My Wilburs are safe from danger with such life-line words as *love, beautiful, yes, joy, pride, wonder* interwoven with every strand.

I am Coyote, the Native American mischief maker who tricks people into learning through playful and delightful ways.

I am Anansi, the keeper of the stories. The Story Box belongs to me.

I am Scheherazade. As long as we tell stories, we will live.

We are canaries in a coal mine. We keep singing as long as the air is good. When the singing stops, the air is poisoned and the canaries are dead. In Room 4 on the Second Floor, the songs and the stories never stop.

I am Sacajaweya helping to guide you through unfamiliar lands. We will make paths and maps together.

I am the blocker in our daily games—trying to keep all obstacles from tackling my team, paving the way for children's touchdowns. I play defense. I'll guard you until you score. In our room, the playing field is flower-sweet, and we are all the cheering section.

Room 4 on the Second Floor is a rainbow room of 36 flavors, not just vanilla and chocolate. It's a can of 57 varieties of human beans. It's alphabet soup. It's an archaeological dig, and we are explorers and scientists together. It's a time machine, and we choose adventures from layers of earth's history. It's a spaceship flying through the solar system—stars everywhere.

Room 4 on the Second Floor is a just-discovered treasure ship. See the journals, letters, sketches, and ship's logs buried in rusty boxes with souvenirs of long-ago journeys.

Come to our rain forest. Listen to the music of insects, animals, trees, and wind. Catch the brilliant throb of colors. Room 4 is an ocean; we understand the language of whales.

Our class is a tribe, a clan, a village, a family. We are together; we speak in a special vocabulary. Like the Hopi, we have no words for hatred and meanness. The Eskimos have many words for *snow*, and in our room we have many words for *love*.

Our room is a welcome wagon. We are Hawaii and greet you with flower leis and ceremonies.

When we arrived at the Emerald City, the preschoolers told me that the Tin Woodsman wanted a heart, the Scarecrow wanted a brain, and Lion wanted porridge.

Porridge! Dorothy! Room 4 on the Second Floor is Kansas and you are home. I am Glenda and Auntie Em, and you'll never have to be afraid again. In this room, you will never be Lost, only Found. Dorothy, we will catch you in our loving web. *Hearts*, *brains*, and *porridge* are the words that keep you safe.

Come play with us! Our room is the hokey-pokey; we put our whole selves in.

My room is Number 4 on the Second Floor.

What's happening in *your* room?

Do only the youngest children learn best through hands-on, direct experiences with meaningful tasks—that is, by handling "stuff"? Effective teachers at all grade levels know that such experiences are at the heart of real learning.

Stuff

Rose Stough schleps shoeboxes and bags full of junk from her basement to her car. What is it? Stuff—like nails, crayons, shells, ashtrays, crushed soda pop cans, clothespins, beans, plastic cups, scraps of fake fur, paint rollers, candles.

Why is Rose hauling this massive collection to school? Hurrying around her classroom, she organizes what she calls, "my five study stations." On each table in each station, she sets a shoebox of stuff accompanied by clearly printed instructions, challenges, and suggestions.

Rose's children work with their neighbors, Marilyn Nelson's fourth and fifth graders, in small science groups to take turns researching in the five stations. For weeks, these peripatetic scholars compare properties of matter: They count, measure, weigh, order, question, sniff, and touch. They discover grams, centimeters, cubic units, volume, and metrics. They learn about solids and liquids. They learn how to make observations and inquiries. They turn a Twenty Questions game into an extension of their studies, guessing objects by asking pertinent questions about their properties.

Rose turns herself into Ms. Wizard and fascinates the children with simple experiments. They find out about the movement of molecules by dabbing cologne on tissues and breathing in the sweetness of the room. They combine baking soda and vinegar and produce carbon dioxide.

For weeks, Rose's room churns with the energy of children looking, labeling, comparing, illustrating, reading, sharing, sorting, talking, and learning. As an extra bonus, they (of course) do great on their science test!

Don't try to phone Rose! She's already busy gathering more stuff to start a study of simple machines for her next science experiences with the two classes. "Got any old wheels, clocks, or gears?" she asks neighbors and shopkeepers as she drops more great stuff into boxes and bags.

According to popular myth, only our very youngest children learn effectively through hands-on, manipulative, concrete, direct experiences related to meaningful tasks; but creative teachers of *all* grade levels know that such activity is the stuff of effective education. It's not enough to study swimming from a chapter in a textbook or from ditto sheets. We need to see, feel, splash, and dangle our toes in *water!*

Make a few waves! Ask the kids; they'll urge you to give them paper, scissors, tape, cameras, maps, yardsticks, blue-prints, compasses, poster board, globes, shoe boxes. "Challenge us," they say. "Invite us into the process. Watch us learn!" Observe children managing school stores, organizing field trips, publishing newspapers, building stage sets, and initiating their own research projects! No matter what our age, our achievement *and* enjoyment are multiplied when we are given an active role in our own learning.

Rose had no trouble understanding another teacher Marilyn Cohen's devastation on discovering that her car had been stolen. Marilyn wailed, "The worse was that all my stuff for Thanksgiving was in it! All my books and stuff for my kindergarten!"

A few days later Marilyn was ecstatic. "The best thing happened! The best thing!" she shouted. "What?" I asked, "They found your car?"

"No," Marilyn bubbled joyfully, "They found my *stuff!*"

Wanting their children to succeed, parents (and teachers!) may do too much pushing. There are simpler, older, more natural ways of enriching children's lives and learning.

I'm Worried About Our Children

I'm worried about our children.

Under the ABCs of *Anxiety*, *Betterment*, and *Competition*, many adults are practicing a kind of push-comes-to-shove child-rearing philosophy that starts programming children for success at birth and, sometimes, even in the womb.

"To everything there is a season" takes on new relevance as we view the disturbing educational approach that boasts of four-year-olds naming the characters from Shakespeare before they learn to love the rhymes and rhythms of Mother Goose, that encourages children to skip by "Twinkle, Twinkle Little Star" and move directly to Beethoven's Ninth. These well-intentioned but misguided parents and teachers forget that children find their own 10 toes without the aid of cards flashing pictures of 10 toes; they crawl without crawling lessons and babble, imitate, sing, and talk without the assistance of computer games.

Those who advocate this speeded-up, adult-directed curriculum look to the lives of such geniuses as Michelangelo, Einstein, and Leonardo. Let's take a closer look at those lives: Michelangelo's parents never encouraged his artistic abilities. Einstein was considered a slow learner. Leonardo spent his life looking for the mother he never knew, achieving his phenomenal accomplishments without strong parental direction. I am *not* recommending discouragement, desertion, or misunderstanding as guarantees of high-achieving offspring! I am just reminding us that children are complex, total beings (in the state of becoming, as we all are). Children begin the world anew with their own unique combination of strengths, interests, originality, courage, imagination, and determination. They are *not* "little sponges" as one new-age parent described in a magazine article.

The most distressing aspect of this system is that it conveys a *closed-up* notion of the world. Parents and teachers who advocate this high-pressure educational philosophy are really giving their children these messages:

• We will provide you with all the answers;

• Learn them and you will succeed; and

• Better still, learn them faster and you will make it sooner than everyone else.

(Why, these children may even hit puberty before kindergarten!)

In this unnatural, high-anxiety setting no room exists for questions, and no slot is reserved for spontaneous discovery, the surprise of exploration, or the excitement of learning. In this scheme of things, it's the product that is emphasized; the process is devalued. Plato believed "the only beginning of learning is wonder." Where does wonder fit into this accelerated, pressure-cooker scheme?

Children are the greatest learners on earth. They can learn anything, any way, and from anyone. But, just what is it that children are learning?

I'm afraid that many "superbabies" are learning how *not* to be children. They are learning before they need to and more than they need to about tension, competition, failure, disappointment, and frustration. Most importantly, they

might be learning that love is connected somehow with successfully performing for parents and teachers. Children who lose their spirit of adventure, their willingness to risk in new experiences, their ability to play with ideas and concepts can be considered deprived, maybe even disabled.

I am worried about our children caught in this acceleration process. Two incidents chosen from a too-ample supply are

1. Do you think Robbie enjoys his lessons? As his fellow kindergartners practice writing their names with feelings of exuberance and pride, he freezes at the touch of a pencil in his hand—terrified to write even his own name because, "What if I make a mistake?"

2. Does first grader Sherry "rejoice in her own works"? Every day she shreds her school papers, calling herself "dumb and stupid." Instead of heeding A.A. Milne's glorious proclamation—"Now I am six and I'm clever as clever; I think I'll be six now forever and ever!"—she stares with deep, sorrowful, defeated six-year-old eyes of failure and says, "I wish I was dead."

I have seen kindergarten children sitting in silent-reading groups working on dittos. I have seen three-year-olds told to redo their Thanksgiving pictures and "do it right! Pilgrims' hats are *black*; don't use any other color. Watch Nancy; she's doing the *best* job!"

When teachers and parents discuss ways of enriching the lives of young children—ways of helping them to *learn to love learning*—the best suggestions are the oldest, most natural, most obvious, most simple. They are so easy that we forget that we already know them:

- Hang loose and relax.
- Talk with your children. Share and compare observations, questions, experiences, wishes, wondering. Laugh together.
- Listen to music of all kinds. Enjoy the music. Let it inspire movement, art, stories, quiet times.
- Read to and with your children. Surround them with stories, poems, riddles, plays. Read to yourself. (What books do *you* love? If you want children to love reading, show them by your example.) Discover the delight of creating your own stories, your own writings. Children already know about this. Keep the flame burning.
- Walk with the children. Walk with awareness. Stop! Look! Listen! Be a person on whom nothing is lost. Martin Buber believed that everything is waiting to be hallowed by you. What do you hallow? A walk around the street with an aware, responsive, sensitive, involved adult is more enjoyable and valuable to a child than a trip around the world with a rigid, closed-minded, authoritarian tour leader.
- Encourage imaginative responses, original thinking, freedom of expression, new experiences. Don't be a critic or a judge. Be a person who rejoices in your own works and the works of others.
- Use the resources at your doorstep: libraries, museums, art galleries, parks, playgrounds, construction sites, gardens, zoos, bakeries, fruit stands, orchards, street signs, parking lots. The word *boring* does not belong in the vocabulary of any child.

Our kids don't need expensive gimmicks, shiny educational tools, designer jigsaw puzzles, video games, and heavy-handed adult intervention in their daily education. Let's not just rely on machines, no matter how great is their potential in the learning process.

Our children need an environment sweetened with tender loving care, encouragement, inspiration, role models, and time—time to play, pretend, explore, experiment, and wonder; time to develop at their own pace and in their own special rhythms. When children learn in such safe, supportive settings under the gentle, constant guidance of loving adults, they prove over and over again that they are among the most creative members of this gifted and talented human family of ours.

Be ready for astonishment. Those of us who have spent most of our lives working with children know that, when we let them, *they teach us* about looking at everyday, ordinary miracles with fresh eyesight and insight. Children take us on a journey to our own beginnings when the world was new and waiting to be discovered again.

We have a lot to learn.

II.

Valuing

the Real

FUNdamentals

Playfulness, humor, joy, and the celebration of learning are the real "basics" that should abound in any environment where children spend their time.

Dear Mrs. Chenfield,
   I liked dancing to all that jazz.
It sure was fun. When we had to
do things with our legs, I got real tired,
those movements sure are neat that we
did.
                              Your friend,
                              Andy

For children, play is as natural as breathing—and as necessary. When children do not get the chance to play for hours each day—and, today, many do not—their physical, intellectual, social, and emotional development is diminished.

"Wanna Play?"

Wanna play?" The most popular question of my childhood!

"Wanna play?" The most welcome invitation of my childhood!

And what did we play? Handed-down games like Jacks, Stick Ball, Kick-the-Can, Statues, Hide 'n' Seek, Stoop Ball, Tag, Marbles, Hopscotch (we called it "Pottsie"), Toss Cards, Giant Steps, Mother May I?, One Potato, Cat's Cradle, Red Rover, Follow-the-Leader, Jump Rope, Allie-Allie-in-Free, bouncing ball rhymes like "*A, My Name Is—.*"

And what else did we play? Made-up games like House, School, Hospital, Zoo, Circus, Jail, Jungle, Detectives, Restaurant, Office, Lost, Castle, Monsters, Blind, Pirates, Invisible, Movie Stars, Heidi, Peter Pan, Wizard of Oz.

And what did we play with? Marbles, tin cans, skate keys, sticks, ropes, string, chalk, stones, dolls that we named.

And what was the magic? Towels tied into capes, ribbons brightened into crowns, sheets draped over umbrellas that became tents, cigar boxes locked into treasure chests.

Contrary to popular myths that children have *short* attention spans, our games went on and on—and on. Sometimes for weeks. Sometimes for months. Sometimes the only way a game ended was when the family moved! Deep down, I think my parents are reluctant to admit that this is the reason our family moved so often.

Our games taught us rules. We learned to interact in meaningful and enjoyable ways; we learned about structures.

Our games taught us different roles. Through improvisation, imitation, and invention we tried on different possibilities; we understood more of the complex interplay of personalities and positions.

Our made-up games taught us exercises—for imagination and positive human relations. As we learned to speak in many voices—tackling challenging ideas and concepts— our language developed. We learned our language by *using* our language in complicated, delightful, and integrated ways.

Our games taught us skills. Our competence grew in physical, social, intellectual, and psychological areas. We manipulated and controlled our environment. We learned how things work. We were *never* bored!

*   *   *

Lately, I've been worrying about our children. Lots of anxious parents are distressed that their children are wasting precious learning time "playing."

"Frills! Frivolous activities!" they say. "In this super-competitive, technological society, we need to start preparing our children at very early ages for success and achievement. There's no time to waste. Let's get back to the basics! Our kids don't need play groups; they need reading groups. They don't need storybooks; they need workbooks. They don't need umbrella-draped sheets; they need ditto sheets."

So many teachers tell me that they are pressured to minimize open-ended, spontaneous, free time for children in favor of formalized structures, tight-fitting programs with predetermined outcomes, constant adult intervention, and strong direction.

They tell me that parents want *scores!* Grades! Tests! If something isn't tested and doesn't have a grade, it doesn't count. It's a frill!

"Cut play!" "Downplay play!" Contrary to these many voices that come down hard on schools and teachers and have often been effective in turning kindergarten play areas into grim study halls, research clearly supports the vital importance of play in the lives of children. From the National Association for the Education of Young Children to the Association for Childhood Education International, virtually all of the professional education organizations have published major policy statements reaffirming the central role of play in child development. Books by leading scholars discuss the loss of play. The titles of two examples indicate strong concern: Neil Postman's *The Disappearance of Childhood* and David Elkind's *The Hurried Child*.

I am influenced by research. But I am also affected by direct observation and experience. From my decades-old collection of countless incidents demonstrating children's love for self-directed, informal, imaginative play, I choose these three to share with you.

• **Ricky's** parents, who are members of the New-Toy-of-the-Day Club, have turned his room into a dazzling display of flashing, computerized, stereophonic, electrical recreation equipment. On the day of our visit, we find Ricky deep in concentrated play. What is he playing with? His new video-computer game? His set of cartoon-inspired transformer characters? His power-driven space station? None of the above. Ricky, head bent forward in intense concentration, is playing with his three favorite toys: a cardboard paper towel roll, a cardboard box, and flexible, bendable straws!

• **Peter** flies into preschool, a towel wrapped around his shoulders.

"Hi, Pete," I greet him.

"I'm *not* Pete," he informs me.

"Who are you?"

"Superman!"

"Well, Superman, we're delighted to have you with us today."

Superman flies through warm-up exercises, zooming across the bridge as we dramatize the "Three Billy Goats Gruff," flashing his cape as he frightens off the Troll.

As we say goodbye at the end of the session, I hug him and wave, "Bye, Superman."

"I'm *not* Superman," he informs me.

Uh-oh, I think to myself. He's probably already changed back to his regular Peter self. "Who are you?" I ask.

"Clark."

What lesson was dramatized to me that morning? *Never underestimate a child's fascination with make-believe.*

• **Chad,** almost four years old, is playing in his front yard with his sitter, Louise, who is watching him nearby. Talking to himself, lost in his story, transfixed in a private segment of his drama, Chad suddenly spurts into action, jumping high in the air. His jump startles Louise, who runs to him anxiously.

"Are you OK? Be careful!"

Chad looks at her, bewildered. What's *her* problem?

"Maybe you had enough outside play, honey," Louise worries. "How about going in and watching your TV program."

Chad looks up at her and advises, "Cool out, Louise."

* * *

In my years of teaching, I have amassed a storehouse of children's observations, evaluations, and blunt comments. The most memorable comment came from a child who tugged at her mother's sleeve as I, a Bronx-born, middle-aged Jewish American, came toward them on a Columbus, Ohio, street. Pointing to me, the child said, "Mommy, that old Indian came to our school!"

The best evaluation came from a group of kindergartners who told their teacher, after our session together, "That Mimi is a very playful girl!"

This "old Indian" would like to quote Chad and urge our anxious American families, intent on pushing and pressuring and lobbying children, and teachers to "Cool out, Louise!"

Finally, this "playful girl" prays that one day all of our children will look back and cherish the memory of an invitation—an invitation to hours of delight, discovery, shared learning, language expansion, and positive human relations—an invitation to gymnastics for the imagination:

"Wanna play?"

Opportunities for movement—so integral to children's learning (and so much fun!)—belong in every area of the curriculum, as we see in the examples of "moving moments" in language arts, math, science, visual arts, and other learning domains.

Moving Moments for Wiggly Kids

These kids are so restless and itchy today I can't do a thing with them!" The exasperated teacher flops into a chair in the teachers' lounge. I'm supposed to work with her class in a few minutes. She wishes me luck as I walk out the door.

"You're not the wiggliest class I've ever seen!" I challenge the group of squirming, foot-tapping third graders. "I've seen far wigglier classes than you. If you're going to wiggle, wiggle with all your might. Can you wiggle without stopping for one entire minute?" I slap the desk 60 times. The children wiggle frantically. When they slow down, I admonish them, "Don't stop! You'll never make the Wiggly Olympics if you slow down!" After one minute, all faces are flushed, eyes are shining.

"Wonder if you can control your muscles, really control them? Your mind is the boss. Mind over matter! *Don't move at all*—not even an eyelash, not even a nostril—for one minute. Heartbeats and stomach growling don't count!"

Sixty beats on the desk. The children are utterly still. Except for a few uncontrollable smiles and eyeblinks, no one moves. Not even the perpetual-motion champions.

"You guys are fantastic!" Before they can relax and stretch, I softly instruct, "Think of all the parts of you that can move. Amazing, isn't it? Out of all those parts, choose just one part of you to move. Have you made up your mind? Ready? Move just one part." I tap a rhythm on the desk for a symphony of moving parts.

"Add another part." Sometimes I use a tambourine to beat the rhythm. Sometimes I clap my hands.

"Think of another part. Isn't this body of ours a phenomenal mechanism?" (I think of the hundreds of thousands of children who in study units on "The Body" read from their books but never once experience the wonder of their bodies in a conscious, joyful way.) We are building movement, part by part. The kids are very excited.

"Here we go! Now move everything that can move!" Some people jump right out of their seats. The room is swaying, bending, vibrating, pulsing.

I clap my hands. "Freeze!" Everything stops. We all sit down again. "What parts of you did you move?" I walk to the board, chalk ready in hand.

In just a few minutes, we have a board crowded with words:

Knees	Arms	Nose	Eyes
Head	Neck	Elbows	Shoulders
Ears	Thumbs	Feet	Stomach
Toes	Eyebrows	Cheeks	Mouth
Wrists	Thighs	Ribs	Hands
Hips	Fists		

The kids gasp. So many words! And special words–all the words are parts of ourselves. Children have an extensive vocabulary of words they know but may not be able to read or spell. Discovering areas of knowledge within ourselves is a valuable and necessary strengthening.

There is one word all children can read, no matter what their ability, achievement, or performance–their own names. Quickly, I write their names next to body words.

Bill	Knees	
Jean	Arms	
Neal	Nose	
Dan	Eyes	etc.

Not a sound in the room. Curiosity and wonder. What's she up to? they think.

This is not the time for drills and skill exercises. This is a time for enjoyment and success for everyone in the room, from reluctant learners to whiz learners.

"Do you see your name?" Silly question! "Next to your name is a word. Don't tell." (Some of the children can't read the word after their name. No matter. In a few minutes they will know that word forever.)

I scoot around the room, stopping at every desk.

"Bill," I whisper, "do you know your word?" He shakes his head.

"Knees," I whisper. He nods. "Don't forget it," and I wink and move on to the next. In less than three minutes, all the children know their words. No fuss. No humiliation. Just a secret meeting, a few whispered seconds in duration.

"Let's have a body warm-up, an exercise session. We'll all be leaders. When your name is called, do something that starts with your word. We'll guess what your word is, then we'll all follow your exercise. Ready?

"Bill, you're first."

Bill grins, swishes his knees back and forth.

"Knees!"

"Right!" We all swish our knees.

Jean's turn. Jean flings her arms in the air and waves them.

"Arms!"

"Right!" We all wave our arms in the air.

Down the list. Everyone is a leader. Everyone guesses the word correctly. Good feeling.

"Let's take five of our words and do something special with them. Which one shall we start with?"

"Toes," someone calls. On another part of the board, I write, My toes——. "Elbows," "ears," "fingers," and "head" are called out and duly written down. We have a word series:

My toes_____

My elbows_____

My ears_____

My fingers_____

My head_____

"Write these five lines on your paper. Each of them needs to be finished. My toes——what? Whatever you want to say. Go on to the next word. I know you can finish the five of them in *one minute*. No, Seth, spelling doesn't count; you can correct them later. Yes, Brett, you will be graded on them. Everyone who writes will have an *A*. OK, begin!"

Heads bent over desks. Pencils scratching. Time's up! You'd be surprised what people can create in a very short time—before they can scratch out and indulge in self-doubt and self-consciousness.

My toes are jelly beans.

My elbows need room.

My ears are pierced.

My fingers are wearing rings.

My head is smart.

— Cara

My toes point out.

My elbows are bent.

My ears hear loud music.

My fingers play chopsticks.

My head gives me a headache.

—Susie

It takes only a few minutes to go around the room and read them all. Each person has an original way of writing, of moving, of seeing. We learn to appreciate our uniqueness and to enjoy sharing. The little "poems" will be rewritten neatly, illustrated, and tacked on the bulletin board as part of a collage on movement. It will be one of the most popular displays of the school year. The "poems" will be the material for choral reading and creative movement and dramatics.

The movement words will be kept in a special spot in the room and added to. The class will do warm-ups every day with names and body parts changed. The whole experience won't take as long as it is taking me to write it out for you, so please don't say, "We have no time!"

Moving is as natural to learning as breathing is to living. We have to be taught not to move as we grow up in our inhibited, uptight society. The older we get, the more self-conscious, the more paralyzed we become.

Movement is a legitimate way of learning. It is *not* a frill. It is *not* extraneous activity that we can cut out of the budget when a bond issue fails. Movement is the way some people learn best; and it lends itself beautifully to successful, satisfying experiences for all participants. Children who rarely succeed will find many opportunities for building a healthy self-image and strengthening self-confidence if movement is used in all areas of the curriculum. The child who can't read or spell or count may lead the class in somersaults, cartwheels, and physical coordination. You, the teacher, need not enroll in the American Ballet Theater or Martha Graham's School of Modern Dance to enrich your curriculum with moving moments. You need not wait till a specialist comes in to encourage your students to move. Stretch your own mind and limbs and commit yourself to the value of movement.

Gwen Marston, enriching the lives of children in Flint, Michigan, had groups of children "show" their spelling words. One group interpreted *volcano* in movement. Another demonstrated *oasis,* and still other children described *earthquake* with their bodies. Learning to spell the words is one kind of learning. Truly comprehending the meanings of the words is another kind of learning. Both are important.

We used masking tape on the floor to create three shapes: a large circle, a large square, and a large triangle. Is your mind buzzing with moving possibilities? Here are a few of the things we did with preschoolers and primary children.

• "Find a shape with a corner and stand in it."

• "Can you make corners with your body?" (Arms stretched out at right angles.)

• "Can a few of you get together and shape yourselves into a corner?" (Bodies stretched along the floor, lined up in perpendicular patterns.)

• "How about all of you together making a huge square with your bodies. Four corners, right?" (Lying down, standing up, sitting down—there's more than one way to make a square.)

• "Somewhere on the floor is a shape with no corners. Can you find it and stand in it?" "There are no corners in a circle!" Douglas shouts, plunging into the middle of the circle. Gleeful, the others tumble after.

• "Can you find circles on your own body? Great! Nostrils! Your head! Wide-open mouths! Excellent!"

• "Can you turn your body into a circle? How would it move? Are there circles in the room?" "The clock!" "The lights!" "The fans!" are called out.

We are surrounded by circles and squares. We turn circles into wheels. We become a merry-go-round. We become a great pizza that goes into the oven and has pepperoni and tomatoes and cheese chunks melting. (Of course, children choose which parts of the pizza they want to be.)

We talk about square shapes, triangular shapes, and circular shapes. We think of square sounds and circular music. We wonder how lines make us feel, how curves make us feel. We walk in lines and curves. We turn our bodies into curves.

We imagine a great jack-in-the-box with a circle as the face, the triangle as the hat, and the square as the box. We turn ourselves into jack-in-the-boxes and crouch down, hidden away, then one-two-three and pop up! What other designs can we make with circles, squares, and triangles? Our world turns into these shapes.

Think of the curriculum as the dry bones in Ezekiel. Until a special spirit is breathed into it, it won't live. It will remain a dry, skeletal structure. If movement becomes a part of everyday learning, related to all areas, not isolated (9:15 A.M. Wednesday—Time for Movement or Creativity lesson—Thursday at two), then the dry bones will grow flesh and form and live. That curriculum will become meaningful, valid, and exciting. All real learning is exciting. The Talmud tells us that "the lesson that is not enjoyed is not learned."

We should keep this thought in mind as we endlessly drill, quiz, grade, and test. What are we testing?

* * *

There is an art show in the multipurpose room. The class files in quietly. The teacher glances quickly around the room, noting various paintings and sculptures. Children stroll around, passing the pictures casually.

"If you see a picture with an animal about to move in it, take the shape of that animal," the teacher instructs.

Suddenly, all the lights go on. Powers of observation and attention shift into high gear. A first grader rushes toward a painting and shapes his body into a pounce. One child after another discovers the painting of the lion about to pounce and imitates the shape.

"Boy, you folks are sharp today! If you find a painting that shows a person hidden inside something and peering out at you, take his shape."

Once again, children look at the paintings with an urgency rarely displayed. Two boys find the picture of the Bedouin squatting in the desert, his face hidden in his robes. The boys squat on the floor, cover faces with arms, and peer out.

Children and I have "moved" to all the art shows available to us and moved to pictures and designs in the class-rooms, as well as museums and community centers. Extend the experience directly into an art, music, social studies, science, or language arts activity.

"Shh! Listen to the painting! What kinds of sounds do you hear?" (In front of the city scene.)

"Doesn't this painting smell delicious?" (Standing before a lush summer landscape.)

There are no gimmicks, no techniques, no guaranteed exercises for you to imitate. Go with the material! Shape it any way you want! Follow its path! Don't close the door on any possibility of breathing life into your lessons.

* * *

How many subjects did you pass in school without having any real understanding of their true meaning? I managed to fake my way through chapters of reading, questions, quizzes, and exams in numerous subjects. Does the following hypothetical lesson indicate any depth of learning?

The Sassafras Nation invaded the Purple Onion Patch in the spring of 1497, resulting in the merging of the Sassafras Nation with the Purple Onion people.

Question: When did the Sassafras Nation invade the Purple Onion Patch?

Question: What was the result of that invasion?

"*A*–plus! You just made the honor roll. Congratulations!" *What is such learning worth? What do we really know when we've completed such a lesson?*

* * *

The Earth rotates on its axis and revolves around the Sun. It takes one year to revolve around the Sun and one day to rotate on its axis.

There are many children who could get an *A* in our test on the solar system, but perhaps, down deep, they don't really understand what it's all about (see the above lesson on Sassafras Nation).

"John, you be the Earth. Can you slowly turn around without getting dizzy? Very good."

"Iris, you be the Sun. You can glow right in the middle of the room. Lovely!"

"Dan, come and be the Moon. Now, what is the Moon's relationship to the Earth?"

"Let's start the Earth and Moon revolving around the Sun as they rotate. Now, add other planets. Don't leave out the asteroids. Our own planetarium! What kind of space music can you think of? What about a rocket ship launched from Earth toward Mars? Certainly, you can be the rocket ship, Roger—flying out beyond the solar system?"

* * *

You can subtract, add, multiply, or divide children. The math example written on the chalkboard can spring to life in the limbs and muscles of your class. Small children can learn their numbers in several ways.

"Watch how many times I do something. Count it and tell me." (Stamp with feet five times.)

"Five?" the children guess. (Hold up a card with the number 5 on it or write it on the board.)

Give each child a card with a number on it and explain, "Keep your own number a secret."

"Howard, do something the number of times your card says, and we'll guess your number." (Howard hops 12 times.) The class has no trouble guessing the number. Howard beams. He holds up his 12. Everyone hops 12 times.

Today, no one will fail in math. Today, we will all make the honor roll. Today is a wonderful day. We are moving! We are learning! We are alive!

* * *

There is no end to possible suggestions or activities. I could tell you about transforming favorite books into movement—how wonderfully classes spontaneously interpret *Make Way for Ducklings, Snow White and the Seven Dwarfs,* or *Where the Wild Things Are.* I won't because I want you to think of moving to your own favorite books. I could tell you how Barbara Reed, a preschool teacher in Columbus, Ohio, celebrated a week of learning about magnetism by constructing a magnet, letting the children turn themselves into different materials, and going around the room with the magnet to see how each material responded to its pull. But, I won't. I want you to think of movement possibilities in all areas of your curriculum!

This essay is not finished—it just stopped for now because we must go on to other things. In the meantime, get moving! Your children are waiting for you and anxious to begin. And don't forget the magic word: *enjoy!*

When teachers feel pressure to conform to teaching practices or agendas different from their own, they may need to become "bilingual"—to speak the educational lingo of the day when necessary, while continuing in their own classroom to speak the "language of the spirit."

There's a Wolf at Your Door

Feeling stressed, overwhelmed, intimidated?

Finding yourself inarticulate, defensive, insecure?

Pulled and pushed by the pressures of persistent criticism, accusations, competition?

Is your flame blowing out?

* * *

I'm here to help.

First, build a house of beliefs and commitments. Don't construct your house out of sticks or straw. Too flimsy! Any wolf can blow it over. Your house of beliefs and commitments must be made out of bricks—a strong, sturdy structure resistant to quaking events, unexpected knocks at the door.

On every windowsill of your house, place signs facing inward. They are for you to read and remember. They state, Bilingual Classroom: Two Languages Spoken Here.

About the bilingual—if your house of beliefs is made of bricks, you are fluent in two basic languages. What are the two languages?

Let's start with the first! This is the language of the *spirit*. This is the vocabulary of adventure, excitement, serendipity, delight, surprise, amazement, imagination, curiosity, experimentation, integration, playfulness, humor. This is the language of the heart. This is the language of the *ear* inside the *heart* (find it?). And, deep within all the hearts, if you listen, you can hear the *arts*.

This is the sacred language of learning in an environment aglow with warmth, love, respect, trust, mutuality, encouragement. In this language the first syllable of fundamentals is celebrated—*fun!* All who come to be with you share the motto the Italian children in the Reggio Emilia program live—Nothing Without Joy. This language speaks the spirit of the wonder of learning. It lights the way for all of your children (all of your prodigies) as you share a special time (never to come again).

The wolf at the door is *not* interested in the Spirit Language. That's why you are bilingual. "So," you may ask, "what kind of language will keep wolves from huffing and puffing and blowing down my house of beliefs (and myself)?"

Wolves at the door demand to know that you know what you are doing at all times. They challenge you to be accountable, clear, concise, knowledgeable, and responsible. They want to know that you are thoroughly conversant in the latest terminology of institutionalized education. In this language, words like *methodology*, *outcomes*, *objectives*, *skillmaster*, *time-on-task*, *assessment*, *standardized testing*, and *classroom management* are high on the vocabulary list. Learn them. Know them. Write them 50 times in your workbook. Use them in sentences.

As you can easily see, this is *not* the language of the spirit.

About wolves—you may ask, "Who *are* the wolves at the door anyway?" The wolf at the door may be a child—a cool, know-it-all, smug, wiseacre kid—"I've already heard *that* on my video. That's *not* the way to tell *that* story!"

Or the wolf may be a colleague —"Don't you think your class needs more . . . more *seat* work? Want to borrow any dittos?"

Or the wolf may be a parent—"Other teachers have *their* reading groups. Why don't *you?*"

Or the wolf may be an administrator—"Just exactly what is going on? The music is so loud and all that laughter—where *is* the teacher?"

Or the wolf could be a community representative—"Clearly, it's because of teachers like *you—frill* teachers—that the levy failed! We'll never catch up with the Japanese with such frivolity! Creativity is definitely *out* of the curriculum in *this* district. Back to the basics!"

Or the wolf might be . . . (can it be?). Oh, no . . . the worst wolf of all—*yourself*—"I couldn't possibly let a puppet give my spelling test. What a stupid idea . . . and frankly, I just don't have the nerve to put silly stickers on the children's work. I'd feel like a laughing stock. . . ."

You may still be a bit confused and about to ask, "Just how can I use this bilingual concept in my everyday real life? Give me a few examples." OK. A couple of examples.

Example #1

About to begin my Artist-in-the-Schools residency, I asked the kindergarten teacher what she was doing that was special. She answered, "The short vowel sound of *ĕ* (eh)."

Thinking she was kidding around, I joked, "Wow! Isn't *that* special?" but she was serious. Because I had brought my tambourine, records, and puppets, her kindergartners were eagerly awaiting the promise of something exciting to happen.

So, we celebrated the color *rĕd*. We turned ourselves into *rĕd ĕlves*. We made up a *yĕll* for *rĕd ĕlves*. In the *yĕll*, we added the wonderful word, *yĕs*. On the *shĕlves* were *shĕlls*. We *hĕld* them to our ears. We did *rĕd ĕlf ĕxercises*.

When we heard the knock at the door and a concerned wolf asking, "For heaven's sake, what's going on here?"—I didn't mumble jumble in tongue-tied incoherence. After all, I speak two languages! I'm bilingual!

I explained, "Through songs, dances, cheers, poems, and designs, we are celebrating *red elves yelling yes* as they *exercise*, and *pet shells* on the *shelves*. Through these delightful activities, we will discover an important sound!" (This is the Spirit Language.)

My friend standing in the doorway looked puzzled. "Huh?"

No problem. Immediately and authoritatively, I replied, "We are learning the short vowel sound of *ĕ* (eh)!"

"Sorry to disturb you," apologized the wolf, closing the door gently as she left.

Example #2

Today Latoya is in charge of the daily Welcome Ceremony that begins each morning. She flips the welcome-chart pages and chooses the one she particularly likes, the one created by the class and marked with words and illustrations to note the sequences. They are (1) Smile, (2) Thumbs Up, (3) Waving Hands, (4) Peace Fingers, (5) Arsenio Hall Circle Swings, and (6) Clapping Hands. Latoya selects reggae music from the Caribbean to accompany the Welcome dance.

As the children greet each other, following their own original choreography of Smiles, Thumbs Up, Waving Hands, Peace Fingers, Arsenio's Circle Swings, and cheery Clapping Hands, there is a knock on the door.

"Could you tell me what's happening in this room?" challenges a wolf standing in the doorway.

I do not hem and haw, shift and hesitate—embarrassed, unsure, insecure. After all, I speak two languages! I'm bilingual!

I explain, "We are sharing our sacred, morning Welcome Ceremony that starts off each day with the feeling of cohesion, of family, of belonging, of sharing, and of immediate success so that we all feel renewed with possibilities and hope." (That is the Spirit Language.)

From the doorway, my friend's expression is one of puzzlement.

"Say what?"

Without hesitation, I add, "We are also practicing listening skills, paying attention, language development, vocabulary recognition, small- and gross-motor skills, cooperative learning, reviewing information, sequencing and patterning, following direction, verbs, multicultural education, leadership, classroom . . . ."

"Please, go on. Don't let me interrupt you." The door is gently closed as the wolf leaves to knock on the door of another house.

* * *

I'm afraid that too many distressed educators, too often, are finding themselves flustered, numb, and dumbstruck by the barrage of hard knocks. I'm afraid that many educators—burned up and stressed out—have built fragile houses of straw, lost the Spirit Language, and are blown over by even the faintest knock at the door, the slightest threat of a knock. Don't let it happen to you!

Because you *are* bilingual, you can explain with intelligence, clarity, and sensitivity to *anyone* who asks "What are you doing?" at any given moment. You *always* know what you are doing.

Keep the language of the spirit, the language of the heart, prominent in the life of your class and the lives of your children and yourself.

Sometimes the Spirit Language is difficult to understand. You can so easily translate the sacredness of the learning into more accessible vocabulary. *Red elves petting shells* may not always do it for people standing in the doorway and asking, "What are you doing?" They are always reassured by explanations like, "The short vowel sound of *e!*"

Consider this essay another brick in your House Made of Bricks. Now, will you be blown over by the next knock at your door? Not by the hair of your chinney chin chin!

Sharing humor and playfulness with children works many wonders. It breaks open and rearranges closed-in ways of thinking, relieves tension and anxiety, and multiplies the fun of learning.

"My Loose Is Tooth!"
— Kidding Around With the Kids

The old folktale goes something like this: At the beginning of time, the Creator was giving out special gifts to each animal. After all the animals received their special gifts, the Creator realized that he had forgotten to give something to human beings. To make up for this oversight, people received the best gift of all—a sense of humor!

Meet Steve Wilson, a clinical and consulting psychologist who calls himself the World's One-and-Only-Joyologist. His favorite motto is If It's Not Fun, I Don't Want To Do It.

Steve easily spouts statistics and research that overwhelmingly support the importance of humor and playfulness in the classroom. He tells us that teachers who encourage laughter in their classes have children who learn quickly, retain more, and have fewer classroom problems. He urges us to see true, healthful humor as a cathartic activity and a way of relaxing, communicating, sharing experiences, keeping brain cells open and charged, learning, comprehending, developing language, and even clarifying values.

But, we say we work with young children! We *know* how easily and enthusiastically they laugh. Their mirth is natural. If they don't "get it," they don't force laughs to be polite. We really don't need Steve's research reports to demonstrate that children's laughter indicates comprehension, imagination, and perception. Because their language is new, young children are constantly experimenting with words and sounds and phrases, often coming up with completely original discoveries that astonish and delight.

* * *

Because our young children have not solidified stereotyped attitudes, their reactions are honest— often expressing powerful insights described in sometimes hilarious terminology.

Asked how she liked her one-year-old brother Max, seven-year-old Saroj thought for a moment, then she answered, "Forty percent."

With a group of kindergartners, I was reviewing ideas from *The Wizard of Oz,* which most of the children had seen on TV that week. I wanted to close in on the tornado as an event to dance about, so I invited the class to think about the tornado as "something that comes at the beginning of the story."

Josh corrected, "It didn't come at the beginning."

"Well, close to the beginning. Early in the story," I continued.

"No," he persisted, "Not at the beginning. The tornado didn't come at the very very very beginning."

"OK. OK. So, what *did* come at the very very beginning of the story?" I surrendered.

"The credits!" he announced.

Most young children have amazing memories and are very loyal to sequential events. Give them time and opportunities to share the way they see things. Not only will you learn a lot about the levels of knowledge unique to each child, but you will have many opportunities to laugh together.

* * *

Often, children's explanations of everyday phenomena are highly original. They help us see connections and relationships that are surprising and refreshing and have their own inner logic. The laughter is often the laughter of surprise and discovery.

We were talking about whistling.

Six-year-old Alicia whispered to me, "Mimi, I'm a very good whistler."

I murmured a response.

"Do you know why I'm such a good whistler?" she asked. "Why?"

"Because I have a bird."

The more I thought about that explanation, the more it soared in my mind. Of course, the hugs and loving laughter that followed warmed both of us. *Laughter is never to make fun of others.* To delight with and share and celebrate together—yes. To ridicule—*no.* The difference makes all the difference.

Back to *The Wizard of Oz.* Another group of children had improvised many of the characters and events in the story through music, movement, and drama. At a rest, I challenged them with the question, "What happened to the Wicked Witch of the West when water was poured on her?"

Jumping up and down, the children shouted, "She melted! She melted!"

Interrupting the group response, tiny Jackie, with the widest, most amazed eyes, rushed to the center and proclaimed in amazement, "Mimi, the Wicked Witch melted in *my* Wizard of Oz, too!"

That was probably the very moment in Jackie's young life when she first realized that she was not at the very center of the universe, that other children shared some of her own experiences, and that they had subjects in common and could have fun together confirming their knowledge. As the new lesson hit her, Jackie "got it." She led the group in merry applause.

* * *

Young children have a logic unique and pure. For example, the subject was "transportation" and the kindergartners and I were gathering suggestions on various means of transportation as material for a dance. During a pause in the group think-tank efforts, I asked, "Does anyone have any more ideas on different kinds of transportation?"

Peter immediately contributed: "Yes, Dad's shoulders!"

In countless, delightful ways young children remind us of things we have forgotten. They keep telling us never to take anything for granted. They continuously make connections even if the connections are expressed in the language they hear.

The story we were improvising had many animals in it. During a rest break, I asked the children to think of any animals that we might have left out of the story. Four-year-old Timmy immediately suggested that "we left out chickmunks!" *Chipmunks* has never sounded right to me since.

* * *

I could go on sharing examples of everyday humor in the classroom that help us remember the delightful surprises in store for those of us who celebrate mirthdays. Children's natural humor based on their interpretations of language, their honest reactions to situations and relationships, their comprehension of ideas, and their original expressions of wonder and curiosity provide daily nourishment of laughter, playfulness, and imagination.

Very little is asked of the adults in the children's lives except to provide numerous opportunities for language interaction and free play and to have the good sense to appreciate the children's contributions.

But here's the *real* challenge: We must become more active participants in the humor process! We must free ourselves so we can enjoy a new way (or is it an old way?) of *being with* our students. Experimental, light-hearted, fun-loving, reassuring—we can be role models, inspirations to our children as we demonstrate through our behavior and our own freedom of speech how to minimize tensions with a joke, how to loosen uptight, closed-in thinking systems—with good-natured kidding, rearranging, and challenging—as we help children expand comprehension, build confidence, and enjoy the learning process.

When we take a more active part in the process, we give ourselves permission to fool around. Try "forgetting" facts. Mixing up information that the children know is guaranteed to foster good-humored fun and high-powered clarification and comprehension. They sure do feel smart!

I always kid the children in some of these ways:

"Let's see, folks, today we're going to review one of our very favorite stories—'Goldilocks and the Seven Pigs.'"

Here are listening skills at work. "WHAT? 'GOLDILOCKS AND THE SEVEN PIGS' You mean——" the children shout.

I interrupt their protests with a twinkly-eyed apology, "Sorry about that, friends. What I mean, let's see, today we're going to review one of our very favorite stories—'Goldilocks and the Three Blind Billy Goats!'"

The variations on this theme are as numerous as ears on potatoes or eyes of corn. I mean—well—you get the idea!

Carrying the fun of mix-up a bit further, I remember the day the children and I celebrated a new turtle puppet I had received as a gift. We improvised a version of the fable "Tortoise and the Hare." We *all* danced the slow, determined, disciplined Tortoise and the fast, jumpy, hoppy, smug Hare.

When we danced the Hare (rabbit), we were so far ahead in the race that we stretched, looked for delicious carrots, and took a break.

As we sat down, munching our invisible carrots, I kiddingly said, "The carrots sat under a tree eating their rabbits." The children rolled over laughing. That line became part of the story, repeated over and over with accompanying giggles each and every time.

When the Tortoise (turtle) won the race, I offered a play on words: "And the turtle wins by a hair!"

One of the children mischeviously added, "The hairy turtle wins by a hair!"

And we ended with—"The Hare lost!"

* * *

When we give ourselves permission to enjoy the playfulness of the creative process, mixing and matching and mismatching, and arranging and rearranging material, we model healthy delight in ideas and relationships. When humor is shared, people feel close and warm with each other. Cohesiveness is strengthened.

Emergency shots of humor can relieve tense situations. Minimize anxiety with laughter.

With yet another group, I celebrated a variation of the "Gifts of the Animals" story. We danced all the animals as they rejoiced in their "gifts." The horses galloped. The birds flew. Kangaroos jumped.

With each new gift, we chorused, "The horses got a gallop. The birds got wings to fly with. Kangaroos got jumping feet." As the story continued, we added to the chant.

In the middle of the drama, I accidentally bumped Avi on the head with my tambourine. His face changed from smiles to whimpers. Tears in his eyes, lips trembly, he stopped the action. Realizing that he wasn't physically hurt, I patted him and said, "And Avi got a tambourine on his head." Avi fell to the floor laughing. The other children joined him in gales of laughter.

Thus the story developed: "The horses got gallops. The birds got wings to fly with. Kangaroos got jumping feet. Avi got a tambourine on his head. Fish got fins to swim with. Monkeys got tricks. Turtles got shells."

And which part of the story did the children most enjoy? The part that turned Avi's lips from a pout to a grin: "And Avi got a tambourine on his head!"

* * *

It's never too late to begin to appreciate and use this very special gift of ours. Remember, we get better at whatever we practice, so begin now to practice enjoying and encouraging the humor within and around you.

Talk with your children and listen to them. When your daily plan makes room for laughter, you will find you and your children learning successfully together in loving ways. Cherish that gift!

Can a Fish Snap Its Fingers?

Can a frog clap its hands?" we ask, clapping.

"NO!" The three-year-olds shake their heads as they clap.

"Can a caterpillar clap its hands?"

"NO!" they chorus.

"But *we* can!" And we do.

"Now we stamp our feet. It's fun to stamp feet. Softly, forcefully! Tiptoe, march! Imagine—we can stamp our feet! Can a duck stamp its feet?"

"NO!" The children stamp.

"Can a mosquito stamp its feet?"

"NO!"

"But isn't it something? *We* can!" And we do.

"Let's snap fingers. Sometimes it's hard for small children to snap fingers. Tickle the air. Brush your thumb. There you go!"

"Snapping fingers is great! Can an elephant snap its fingers?"

"NO!" *Snap. Snap. Snap.*

"Can a kangaroo snap its fingers?"

"NO!"

"Can a fish snap its fingers?"

"My fish can!" one little boy announces proudly.

* * *

We begin with the wonder of it. Whether we're a class of three-year-olds, junior high wisecrackers, or forgotten residents in homes for the aged, we begin with the wonder of it—that we can move.

In classrooms, gyms, all-purpose rooms, basements, recreation rooms, in homes for the aged, meeting rooms in community centers, hospital wards, church and synagogue halls, we have moved with fellow humans from 2 to 102.

Ideas for moving are infinite. We have even scratched careful plans in order to use an idea-of-the-moment contributed by an eager child in spontaneous conversation. We even change lessons for birthdays.

"Dotty is five today." Dotty proudly smiles.

"Well, folks, we have to do something special for a birthday, don't we?" And we junk our scribbled notes for the day. "How many other five-year-olds are there?" Half the class raises hands. "How many are going to be five?" The other half responds. "Five is a super-good number. Let's do everything in fives for our birthday child. What can we do in fives?"

"We can jump five times!" Sandy says. We jump five times. We run five times. We skip five times. We hop on one foot five times. We spend our session rolling, crawling, leaping, sliding, marching, twirling, spinning, bending, stretching, wiggling, flying, somersaulting—*five times*. Dotty leaves glowing. She is thoroughly, deeply five now. In all her limbs and muscles.

Ideas. Ideas. You don't have to be complicated. You don't need a doctorate in dance to enjoy a simple movement.

* * *

"How many ways can we go from this end of the room to the other? I bet we can find 25 ways!" The class doubts.

"What's one way we can cross the room?"

"Walk."

"Right on! Let's walk."

"What next?"

"Skip."

"Good for you! OK, let's skip. That's two ways. Twenty-three more to go!"

The children think of 25 ways easily. The class is over, and tired children are still shouting suggestions into the air like confetti.

"Skip backwards?"

"Slide?"

"We can think of 50 ways easily, can't we, Mimi?"

* * *

We dance every animal. Children love animals. They hop like rabbits, roar and run like lions, stumble like new deer, gallop like horses.

We talk about caterpillars turning into butterflies. I share my son's long-ago question, "Do caterpillars *know* they're going to turn into butterflies?" The children drift with the thought. We imagine how it would be to be a caterpillar who mysteriously and magically and scientifically becomes a new creature. We feel it in our bodies. We sleep in our dark cocoons, curl into ourselves. Great silence is the music of the room. Silence and metamorphosis. A soft drum beat begins our change. Beautiful butterflies of every color and size emerge. Even the roughest boys sprout wings and float gently. The room brightens.

"When I see a butterfly next summer," Debby whispers, "I'll know just how it feels."

Dear Mimi
Thank you for showing us all of the neet stuf. I liked the part when we were Rabbits. I liked when you said a baby comes in from the hospiltly he does not say Whats for lunch

Your Freind

Michelle

* * *

"Christopher Robin goes hoppity, hoppity, hoppity, hoppity, hop. . . ." We sing-song the poem. The children do not need to be told. They hop. And hop. And hop. ". . . Whenever I tell him politely to stop it, he says he can't possibly stop."

We move from being the smallest dots imaginable to the hugest giants. We bounce like balls and turn into elves, witches, and fierce kings; bears searching for honey and escaping from bees; chicks cracking through shells, skaters skidding; basketball players dribbling; circus clowns tumbling; acrobats balancing; and snow shapes melting.

* * *

We stay very still. Now move just one part. Move another part. And another. The miracle of the moving parts. Now move two parts of you. Another two. Now three—four—five—!

We make Thumbelinas with our thumbs and watch them dance. We dance all the toys in the toy store: windup toys that spurt to action, then slow down; cars, trucks, trains, planes; limp rag dolls that leap into limp rag-doll dances; fluffy soft toys that make everyone feel wonderful.

We imagine the sounds our bodies would make as they move. We make the sounds of a finger wiggling, a head shaking, feet kicking, a back bending, arms waving.

We wear a "happy-face" button and wonder how we would move if we were "happy faces." How would a happy face move shoulders? Arms? Heads? Feet? How would a happy face dance?

* * *

With older boys and girls, we play with challenges. Go from up to down in chunks, in pieces. Falling apart. Smoothly. Fiercely. Bounce down! Collapse!

Go from down to up, reaching. Grasping. Pleading. Chopping. Expanding. Untangling. Unwinding. You can do downs and ups forever and never run out of variations. Turn your body into a giggle, into a cheer. A whimper. A whisper. A scream. A warning. A moan.

Make three different body shapes for

Work	Welcome	Hello	Play
Goodbye	Friend	Help	Enemy
Warm	Cold	War	Peace

Anyone who can move can make body shapes, body designs. Pretend you're the design of a poster for those ideas. Work alone or in groups. Work one idea with another, one against another.

Join groups together to make a machine of bodies. Each contributes to part of the machine. The machine has moving parts. It stops and starts. Some parts go fast, some slow. Sometimes the whole machine moves from place to place.

* * *

We talk about refugees. Refugees of time. People leaving the known and familiar, leaving beloved places and things. Gathering immediate necessities and moving directionless to strange lands. We wonder how it feels to be lost and wandering, with no roots. We feel it in our bodies—the heaviness of it, the vagueness of it, the forlornness of that painful situation. We move with no focus, no aim. Some move alone—slowly, falteringly. Some move with others—protective, close together. Through moving we can feel.

The newspaper features a story about a Florida Native American chief who was called on to perform a rain dance after scientists had failed to end a drought. The chief danced and lo, it did rain. We talk about ritual dances, a form of movement transcending time and cultures. Dances for good crops. Dances to ward off evil. Dances of blessing. Dances of warning. Dances of growing. Dances of healing. Everyone chooses a dance. Each improvises. The improvised ritual dances are as effective as any witnessed on a stage. We are awed by the discovery of our own creative depths.

There's no end to ideas. Wherever you are, ideas fall around you. Pick them. Take them. Change them. Use them. Listen to the children and listen to yourself. To move is native to human beings.

Every teacher knows that in a classroom climate of trust and warmth, where no child is threatened and each feels important, respected, and welcome, joyful education is possible. Movement can be a joyful experience that all may share.

* * *

This morning the sky was grim gray. Wind and rain whipped the wet streets. My car stalled and sputtered on the way to the center where I have three classes of preschoolers and one class of adults. In each preschool class, we danced storm. Some of us puffed up like heavy storm clouds, gathered together, and hid the sun. The sun tried to show

through, but we clouds wouldn't let it. Thunder roared. Some of us moved like thunder, roaring and rolling around the room. Rain poured down. We scattered rain with arms and fingers in a lightning jab. We jumped into the air. Wind blew. We huffed around the room, whirling and spinning. Small animals hid from the storm. Birds huddled in feathers. Squirrels rushed to trees. Turtles pulled in their heads. The children were rain, clouds, lightning, thunder, birds, wind, squirrels, and turtles. One little girl lay still on the floor.

"What are you?" I whispered as storm movement raged around us.

"I'm a puddle," she replied.

The storm blew over. The group moved from one end of the room to the other. The heavy puffed-up rain clouds softened into fluffy, floating clouds. The sun shone through. All the little animals sniffed, crawled, flew, yipped, or ran to the sunny air. Happiness beamed on every face.

* * *

This afternoon as I left the center, the clouds were breaking up. The sun burst through. Now as I write, the sky is clear. The air is still. The colors of the day are shining.

I know the scientific explanations of storms, but I also know the magic of dance. I know in my toes that this morning 40 three-year-olds and one middle-age adult exorcised the rain from the day.

The telephone rings. The mother of one of the three-year-olds must tell me, "Randy is convinced that he caused the sun to shine today."

We begin and end with the wonder of it. That we can move.

III.

Tuning in

to Children

Children will teach us how to reach them if we tune in to what delights them, intrigues them, makes them laugh. What we need to learn above all is to "hang out" with children.

Dear Mrs Chenfield,
Thank you
for letting us
have so much
fun.

Your freind,
Jake Shafer

41

Just by tuning in to children—what they like, the words they use, what's going on with them— a teacher gives them the precious gift of acknowledgement and respect. And the learning takes off from there.

On Becoming Teacher Experts:

"Super Girl Is *Not* From 'Masters of the Universe'" and Other Things I've Learned From Kids

When God gives you a music maker like Herbie Hancock, you make up a story about a toy machine factory and try it out one fine spring day, with preschoolers waiting for you at the Leo Yassenoff Jewish Center's Early Childhood program in Columbus, Ohio.

First, we talked about machines—what they're about, how their different parts contribute to the whole process. Then we experimented, turning our arms, legs, shoulders, eyes . . . all of our fantastic body parts into mechanical movements. Break-dancing kids were in their glory! After we warmed up, oiled up, got ourselves in gear, and turned on our power lights, I started a little story and asked the children to turn their bodies into toy machines. Each body was to produce its own individual toy.

"Of course, these toys will be wind-up toys," I suggested.

"Battery-run!" a four-year-old voice corrected.

"Battery-run they are!" I always agree with the children. I'm a cave person caught in the modern world.

The first toys we manufactured with our body machines were battery-run rabbits. What a delight to see rabbit shapes emerge from the flurry of mechanized, individualized choreography created by the children to Herbie's mechanical-sounding music. Once the rabbits were formed, their batteries were turned on and they turned into very hoppity rabbits. We had to be sure these toy rabbits could be sent to any country in the world (to help balance the trade deficit!), so we had to check out their ability to hop to African music for the African market, Israeli music for the Israeli market, Arabic music for the . . . well . . . we're getting away from our story.

Our toy machines manufactured airplanes, cars, and horses. While the battery-operated horses were galloping around the room, testing their Appalachian music, their teacher Michele Gibson Sanderson whispered to me, "If you really want to turn the kids *on*, ask them to make a 'Masters of the Universe' toy."

I must confess that, yes, I had heard of "Masters of the Universe," but, no, I really wasn't tuned into the program and so knew nothing about the characters or plot. But, why should almost total ignorance stop me after all these years?

"We have time for one more toy, gang. Let's see. Hmmmmm . . . what about a 'Masters of the Universe' toy?"

The class exploded into a storm of Fourth of July fireworks! Jumping, clapping, shouting, squealing with excitement, the children waved their arms, calling out:

"I'm gonna be He–Man!"

"Me too! He–Man! No, Ram Man!"

"I'm gonna be Teela!"

"Skeletor! Skeletor!"

I listened, nodded, agreed, and encouraged. This is the verbal and nonverbal outpouring of enthusiasm whenever you offer children choices and decisions based on their loves. In the midst of this celebration of exciting ideas, four-year-old Beth squeaked, "I'm gonna be Super Girl!"

"Fine, great, OK . . ." I continued my supportive murmuring. Then, just as I hushed the group so we could begin the toy machines, Katy walked over to me—eyes deadly serious, index finger on my cheek—and stopped the action by pronouncing:

"Mimi, Super Girl is *not* from 'Masters of the Universe'!"

Silence. The little Super Girl's face fell. I whispered to Katy, "Let's let it slide just for now. Let's let Super Girl be in the 'Masters of the Universe' factory just for today, OK?"

Grimly she agreed but, I know, didn't approve. Before the group I added, "Super Girl has always loved 'Masters of the Universe' characters! She's so excited to be included today."

Our machines went to work. Skeletors, Cringers, Ram Men, Battle Cats, Teelas, Prince Adams, and one Super Girl sprang into very specific, concentrated movement as their batteries were turned on.

Later as the kids left, lifting their faces for a kiss from my puppet Snowball, Katy stopped. Once again her tiny index finger pressed into my cheek, her eyes bored deeply into my own. She might as well have added, "Watch my lips" as she slowly repeated, "Mimi, remember, Super Girl is *not* from 'Masters of the Universe'!"

* * *

We could talk for weeks about lessons to be learned from this 20-minute class session. One of my favorite sayings comes from Norma Canner, a movement educator: "I came to teach and I stayed to learn." That happens often when you teach in "the key of life."

Here are a few things that I learned that day. (I really already knew them, but I guess I just forgot for the moment.)

Children have their own magic vocabularies. Creative, aware, caring teachers know that their students are incredible resource centers. Michele knew how much her children loved the TV program, "Masters of the Universe." She was tuned in to their lives—their interests, hobbies, and favorites (foods, colors, numbers, words, programs . . .). The mere recognition, acknowledgement, and respect for the magic vocabulary of the children yielded immediate, amazing responses. It always does! In classes where teachers teach in "the key of life," the vocabularies and interests of the kids are as relevant, even more relevant, than the lists of words in books that don't know those children.

Children don't learn their language in silence. In classes where education is celebrated as an exciting, unique, dynamic process, and the children are hallowed as special, original human beings (not baked beans or soy beans or green beans), the sounds of their voices are part of the music of the room. Their voices express more than the rote answers to closed-up questions: When was the War of 1812?

Children have a lot to say— in classes taught in the key of life. They have numerous daily opportunities to contribute ideas, observations, questions, experiences, corrections, suggestions, and feelings to the life process of the group. They are never put down, never humiliated. Their opinions and contributions are held in high regard. Creative teachers see the myriad of possibilities in one word. Show it! Tell it! Draw, sing, play, improvise, spell, move, pantomime, sculpt, dance it. Turn it into a story, a riddle, a ballad, a play. Each

idea begets another. Ideas always multiply. There's always more, more, more. The best question is What else? The only limitation is time.

* * *

When Bill Palmer summarized with his Bellingham, Washington, first graders all the punctuation marks they had studied that year, he tossed out to them the questions he always asked his children: "Well, any other ideas? Did we leave out anything? Anything else on your minds on this subject?"

Six-year-old Bonnie raised her hand and in a voice as clear as a bell she told Bill, "You left out the AWK."

Bill raised his eyebrows in a questioning look. "AWK?" He thought for a moment, then apologized, "Bonnie, I don't quite remember the AWK. Could you tell us a little about it? When do you use it?"

"After you write a MAD sentence," she explained.

"Could you show it to us," he asked. She drew an AWK on the board.

Bill gave her his total attention. Then he explained, "In all my reading, I don't think I ever remember seeing an AWK."

Bonnie reprimanded him, "If you had read my journal more carefully, you would have observed that I used an occasional AWK." And so he reread her journal. And so she had.

* * *

When I asked a group of three-and-a-half-year-olds if they knew what caterpillars turned into, Jordan proudly offered, "Butterflowers."

That wasn't a silly answer. It was a wonderful, imaginative answer that conveyed a whole new set of images to our needy minds. Of course we straightened Jordan out, but we did conclude that his butterflowers were every bit as fascinating as butterflies. Personally, I'm in awe of both.

*   *   *

This is my 30th year of teaching. I have learned so many things from my children. The sounds of their voices in classrooms, hallways, lunchrooms, playgrounds, gyms, and restrooms are part of my symphony. Their words on notes, journals, letters, reports, scraps, and doodles are part of my library.

From Donald, the alphabet child whose name was followed by every combination of letters that spelled *failure*, I learned the names, cities, players, and scores of every football team in the professional leagues of this country.

From Cliff, I learned the history of and words to every Bruce Springsteen song.

From Dan, I learned (but still don't understand) how to fly.

From Cara, I tried to comprehend tie-dying.

From Jim, I learned about glass blowing.

From Kira, I learned to say "I love you" in German and in sign language.

From Jeffrey, I learned how to do the Moonwalk.

From Douglas, I caught a glimpse—in his words—of the "fan-tas-omatic" vocabulary of Dungeons and Dragons.

From Debby, I learned all the "nice words."

From Jordan, I discovered butterflowers.

From Bonnie, I discovered the AWK.

And, from Katy, I learned that Super Girl is *not* from "Masters of the Universe."

In this kindergarten class one finds children busily engaged in a host of emerging literacy activities and other learning experiences—and a teacher whose love and respect for each child is evident.

"Thank You for Teaching Me About Rich Words"

When children enter the magical world of Mary C. Byrne's half-day kindergarten, they never have to sit and wait. They are invited to come in, hang up their coats, and "go ahead and get started" in a "work choice."

Some of the "work choices" in Mary's room are reading a story, writing in journals, housekeeping corner, clay, painting and colored markers, big and little blocks, puzzles, dress-up, music center, math center, and science center.

After a half hour of individual choices, the group gathers for discussions, stories, or playful challenges, such as mystery sentence. Mary writes a mystery sentence on the board, softly saying the letters as she writes them, modeling letter writing. An example of one of the sentences is: Today is Jennifer's birthday. Yea! Mary says the words as she writes the sentence.

Then, the gang will play a word game. Mary erases one of the words of the sentence. The children remember that word and, letter by letter, back on the board it goes. The sentence is presented whole, broken down, and recreated. This process helps the children remember the letters.

Mary's students enjoy the best of children's literature. Authors and stories are read, discussed, illustrated, and appreciated. "Oh! What a *rich* word!" Mary stops constantly to admire especially unusual or descriptive language in stories of conversations. Mary loves rich words!

Mary believes that her students are reader–writers. She deeply respects their own resources and experiences; but, the children need convincing. It takes Mary about a week to convince them that they are, indeed, readers and writers. She reminds them of words they know, like their own names and *yes* and *no* and *OK* and *bingo* and *go*.

In Mary's class, every child receives a journal. "Pictures always come first. I write the words they dictate to me under their pictures. After a while, I turn the writing over to them."

Many of the children are afraid to take over the writing. "Oh, you know how to do it," Mary encourages. "C'mon, take a risk!" She prods, nudges, reassures, reminding the children of their many accomplishments that took courage and determination.

"Not to worry!" She reminds them that they're in kindergarten and no one in the world expects them to know how to write and spell every word correctly—"heavens, no"—but, when they begin writing everything they want to say in their journals, their handwriting and spelling will improve day by day.

And they do. And it does.

One outstanding day was the *ing* day. At group time, a few children wanted to know how they could write *looking* or *walking*, so Mary introduced them to *ing*. Such excitement! The children exploded with stories and ideas.

Mary's kindergartners are constantly aware that they are involved in a process. As they write in their journals more and more every day, they articulate their comprehension and growing mastery of written language. "When we jot down ideas in our journals," Mary explains, "we call that *prewrite*. If we especially like a piece, we work on it a little—revise it, polish it up, and get it ready for a book. The children make hand-bound books with pages. They have title pages and illustrations and, believe it or not, many of the children cut out a pocket and paste it on the first page with an original library card inside!"

"Then—yea! author's chair!" Mary continues.

"When the children complete their books, they take their turns as celebrity authors, sitting in our special author's chair with the circle of classmates gathered around. After the story is read, we have a kind of talk show, asking questions about the writing, the story, the ideas."

* * *

Mary is a gifted teacher. One of the children in her class wrote a book for her and presented it the last week of school. It is five pages long, packed with sentences, and is one of Mary's dearest gifts. This is the text of Lindsay's book to Ms. Mary C. Byrne (translated into the boring, standard English of adults):

I love you, Ms. Byrne. I remember the time I was scared. That day I got very used to you. I knew I was going to like kindergarten. We went outside and I had fun. Then we came inside and we had snack. Then we had a little work choice. I played with Kelly and Lee. We had fun. Then it was time to go home.

When I got home I found some balloons on my front stoop of my front door. They said *Lindsay* on them. I was happy because I had never had some balloons with a basket. Jeffrey had two balloons in baskets.

Some things I like in kindergarten are snack and recess and work choice. I like how you let us take our shoes off and I also like how you taught me to read and write and also how I make new friends.

Thank you for teaching me about rich words. I remember when I did not put *ing* on the ends of my words because I did not know how to spell *ing*. And you taught me how to spell *ing* and you taught me how to take a risk.

I remember when I first wrote in my journal, you told me to draw flowers in my dress. I liked when you let me take the sheet of paper to the office that said who was absent and said if everyone was there.

I liked how you let me get the mail. I liked how you let me go to the teachers lounge to get your purse.

I told Mom the other day that I wanted to stay in kindergarten but Mom said I had to go on. I'm glad I had you for a kindergarten teacher. I wish I could stay with you. I will always love you even when I'm in first grade and even when I'm in sixth grade.

Ms. Byrne, I love you. I wish I did not have to leave you.

—*Lindsay*

Thenk you for Teching
Me aBawt rooh WrDs
I re MamBrwan I
DID NOT Per ing
on The end of my wrDs
BeeCKS I DiD NOT NOW
haw to SpL ing AnD
You ToT me haw to
SpL ing AnD You
ToT Me haw to Tack
4 rasck I remaMBr
wan I Frso roT iv
my JrnL You ToLD
Me to Por FLowrs in
my Drrs

ToLD mom The OThr
That I WonTD
sTa iN KonJr gooin
mom sioD I haD
Go on I'm gLowD
haD you for A
Ndr gooN Techr
Wash I LoD sTa
Ble. You I wow alwas
You evav wan im
graD AnD evaN wan
iN g grad Ms Byrne
Love You I wash I
NOT haf to Lev

Our best moments as teachers or parents are likely to come when we stop, look, and listen to children, when we walk along the trail with them—experiencing the "everyday, ordinary, extraordinary life of the child."

On the

Trail

With

Jackie

Three fantastic early childhood conferences in a row—in Mississippi, Georgia, and Massachusetts. It's hard to land! Conferences are heady events—north, south, east, and west, wherever we gather we are warmed by the camaraderie, the sharing of ideas, and the exchange of energies and experiences. Teachers and other caregivers renew their commitment to the healthy, joyful, successful learning by our children and the search for the best ways to accomplish these goals.

With a head dizzy from too many excellent ideas, I bid farewell to friends at the New England kindergarten conference and drive to a close-by town to visit my nephew and niece and their family. Still glowing from the stimulating conference event, I try to tune in to gathering updated family news. Grandma Marilyn has just received another honor for excellent teaching. Grandpa Herb has sold another house. My nephew Seth, the biologist, talks about his research. My niece Zee, the chiropractor, helps me adjust. The three-month-old twins, Annie and Michelle, are aware, perky, and cuddly. Jackie, three years old, shows me dolls, toys, blocks, and dances. Her brown eyes sparkle, and her long, brown ponytail swishes as she runs and skips around the house. It's a sunny but chilly Sunday in November.

"How about a walk?" I suggest.

The babies are sniffling, so Seth and Zee propose a walk just for two, Jackie and me.

"Be sure to take Mimi on the trail," Jackie's dad calls.

Proudly, Jackie puts on her snowsuit by herself, pushing her arms through the sleeves, zipping, and velcroing. I tie the strings on her hood. Patiently, she fits her hands into her beautiful purple mittens.

"Hold hands!" Jackie's mitten takes mine as we step out the back door.

The backyard is bordered by clumps of bushes and trees and rocks. A small stony hill that Jackie calls her "mountain" leads to the property of the family next door. We follow the trail—a tiny pathway zigging and zagging around and across the "mountain." Such a small area! So much to see! What an adventure!

"Look! Red berries. And yellow ones!" Jackie points excitedly to the berry bushes. "Want to see my favorite color berries?" She touches the rust-colored bushes. We study the different colors of berries gleaming so brightly in the clear autumn day.

An experienced hiker, Jackie warns, "Don't run on the trail. Be careful!"

We sit on the mountain looking up at the bare branches of trees outlined against the pure blue sky. I pull Jackie closer to me and steer her focus skyward, "Look up there at the squirrel's nest. See it?"

She squints, blinks, searches the branches. Suddenly, wide-eyed, she shouts, "I see it! A squirrel's nest!"

We look for squirrels' nests in all the surrounding trees. We find four. Big cheers for squirrel nests! Small cheers for bird nests. Bird nests are smaller.

Continuing our journey on the trail, we note twigs and branches that form the shape of alphabet letters. So many *Y*s. *Y* is for *yes*! Nature is always saying yes to us! Jackie finds a twig in the shape of a *J* for Jackie. *J* is for *jumping*. She jumps with excitement, singing: "*J* for Jackie. We found a *J*, a *J* for Jackie!"

Hippity-hoppity along, we find number shapes in twigs, branches, acorns, and nuts. Letters, numbers, berries, nests— we search and count and sing our discoveries.

Now we have walked to the front of the house.

"How about walking up the street?" I ask. Jackie's house is at the foot of a hilly street. She takes my hand.

"Just a little walk, not a big one," she says.

"OK."

"Maybe we'll find more nests to see in the trees," and she lifts her eyes to scan the high branches. Migrating birds fly over us.

"Jackie, see those birds flying together? Looks like they may be flying to the south where it's warmer."

"All of them? All the birds," she wonders.

"No. Some birds stay here and some fly away for the winter."

"Why?"

I admit ignorance. (The poet Theodore Roethke wrote: "Our ignorance is so colossal that it gives me a positive pleasure to contemplate it.")

"Good question. No one really knows the answer to that yet. Maybe when you grow up, you'll be a scientist and will find out about the birds' journeys. Meanwhile, we'll have to watch them and study them."

"I always study the birds," she says. "And the nests," she adds. She stops, looks back, smiles. "There's my house." A purple mitten points down the hill. "I see my house," she sings.

We jump over pebbles, watching our shadows and admiring clouds. Jackie likes the cloud with the feathery tail. I like the cloud that looks like a woolly lamb. "This is a beautiful day," Jackie says. I heartily agree. She stops, looks back, and smiles. "I still see my house!" she sings.

We continue up the hilly street. Overhead an airplane writes jetstream messages in the sky. "Hi, airplane!" Jackie's purple mitten points upward.

We sing her favorite songs from *Peter Pan*, *The Wizard of Oz*, and Raffi and Ella Jenkins. I sing my favorite line from Ella's songs, "Stop, look and listen. Listen to what children have to say. . . ." Jackie knows the words to so many songs. (I am always amazed at the lyrics in the repertoire of young children.)

Jackie shows me what they taught her in school. "Stretch and bend," she describes as she demonstrates.

She likes my earrings. I like her ponytail ribbon. We talk about colors, clothes, babies, and stories. We are almost to the top of the street.

When Jackie turns back to look down, she doesn't smile. Her house is too far below to see. It's out of sight. With a tremble in her voice and an urgency in her grasp, she pulls my hand.

"We need to go back to my own house now."

"No problem," I reassure her. Down the street we steer to Jackie's house, singing a new happy-to-be-almost-home song, doing a jump-along dance down the hill. As Jackie's house appears, her smile reappears.

Up the front steps, banging on the door, she calls, "Mommy! Daddy! We were taking a little walk, but it was a big walk!"

She hops into the house, unzipping, untying, peeling off mittens and sleeves, chattering excitedly. "We saw four squirrels' nests! We went on the trail and up the mountain and found *J* for Jackie and saw birds flying and red berries. . . ."

Later, when my visit ended, she kissed me good-bye and whispered a request, "Next time, can we go for another walk?"

* * *

Without doubt, those three weekends of superlative conferences formed the highlight of my season—every one of them a peak experience. Information, stimulation, inspiration, and motivation—whirlwinds of wonderful ideas, materials, and activities.

In the center of that swirl, though, I found the eye—the calm spot. There in the center of it all I see Jackie hiking along her trail, climbing her "mountain," exploring the boundaries of her world as courageously and creatively as did explorers of old. Brave and scared, cocky and cowardly, she ventures out. Naming and singing, dancing and running, wondering and wandering, she makes reunions and discoveries. There, in the midst of our storm of educational strategies and systems, here is the *everyday, ordinary, extraordinary life of* the child.

Young children don't attend conferences, courses, or inservice training. They leave philosophizing, researching, and analyzing to grown-ups. Young children have better things to do with their time! Sometimes, they're lucky. Loving and caring adults encourage them, help them design and sculpt their world—making trails out of backyard bushes and mountains out of small hills—and help them make sense out of life, out of their lives.

While we rush to workshops and exhibits, lectures and demonstrations, the children are busy finding new vocabulary to fit new experiences, practicing comprehension, seeing connections, and meeting new relationships as their world unfolds and reveals itself to them.

I see us walking along the trail with the children. In the eye of the storm, only a few basic, simple questions need be asked.

What do we do? (All education, training, systems, and strategies count for little until they are shaped into action.)

How are we with the children? (Our beliefs shape our behavior. Do we connect? How do we relate to the children? One-on-one? Two-by-two? To a class? To a school?)

When we "Stop, look and listen—listen to what children have to say," as Ella Jenkins sings so beautifully, and share our minds and hearts with them (a true exchange)— enjoying and exploring together—we find that walking along the trail with our children is the greatest peak experience of them all!

We will enjoy children more and serve them better, as teachers and friends, when we come to appreciate the joys of just "hanging out" with them—experiencing life through their eyes and ears.

Hangin' Out With the Muffin Man

Our Len has so many friends. Michelle is three, and she's called "Shellie Bellie" or "Boo." Harry's two. His folks call him "Baby Mon," "Harry Mon," "H Mon B Mon," "The Hairmeister." Louis is one. His grandpa and grandma call him "Babalulu" or "Luigi." Callie Rose is five months old. Her daddy calls her "Callie Callie Coo." Len is almost nine months old. He's called "Yummy," "Bunny," "Diddle," and "Munchkin"; but our favorite nickname for him is "The Muffin Man," and our favorite activity is Hangin' Out With the Muffin Man.

There are so many things to see when you hang out with the Muffin Man. Big things like buildings and cars. Little things like buzzing flies, eyes changing expressions, a leaf swaying in the wind. Faraway things like clouds. Close-up things like noses. Exciting things like a traffic lights or baggage riding along the airport conveyer belt.

Hangin' out with the Muffin Man is a festival of sounds. He listens to sounds that we hardly notice: the beginning of breezes, mobiles swinging, faucets dripping.

Life is at our fingertips when we're with the Muffin Man because he reminds us about the fun of touching. Fingers want to hold other fingers, spoons, or flower petals. If he can reach it, he wants to touch it. He grabs at dust particles shining in the bright noon, window light and the flickering of passing shadows.

The Muffin Man thinks that the world is a big red ball waiting for him to grab and bounce, to taste and touch. Everything is on the

Muffin Man's menu: dirt, sand, paper, crayons— even food.

Strollering along with the Muffin Man, we talk about so many things. We don't want to miss a second of seeing and being on a walk with, on a talk with, the Muffin Man. It's singing and seeing and saying as we walk with the Muffin Man, chanting names of animals and objects, turning dogs and cats into songs and rhymes and games.

Oh, the patience, persistence, and courage of the Muffin Man! Sitting, crawling, standing, walking. Trying and failing. Pushing and falling. Up, then down, then up again and up, up, *up*, and down and *up*. Pouts and smiles. Whimpers and laughs. Now, we clap hands. "Peek-a-boo, Muffin Man!"

We lull the Muffin Man to sleep after a splashy giggle bath, after hugs in fluffy towels and kisses to shiny clean toes and dimpled fingers, after snuggles and whispers of love, after lullabies and stories and pats on the tush to send him off to sleep with the touch of reassurance. While the Muffin Man sleeps his deep, dreamy sleep in his crib of rainbow colors; in his room of stars, moons, and animals; near his open box of books and toys; we rock in the rocking chair and think about the future.

In a few months Harry starts a new preschool. Michelle will go to a three-day nursery. Louis will try a play group. Len and Callie may be in child care. Some of these children's new friends will also have funny, affectionate nicknames given to them by doting families. Some will have to be given funny, loving names by the new family of friends they share in their caregiving programs, and who may be the first and only people ever to hallow them.

But all of our children are coming to *you*, to school. They will zigzag up the ladder from child care to preschool to Head Start. They will hopscotch around from a family child care home to nursery school to play group. On to kindergarten, to first grade, and on and on along their journeys, along their paths—from our arms to your arms.

One day you may look up to see a group of children standing before you. Check their names on your roster. Check their knapsacks of unique experiences, talents, and gifts. In the sweet circle of your warmth, they're sure to fall in love with you.

Lucky you to be spending time with The Hairmeister, Boo, Luigi, Callie Callie Coo, and their friends and hangin' out with the Muffin Man.

IV.

Teaching From the Heart

At the core of all education that makes a difference in children's lives—beneath all the methods, materials, and curricula—is a teacher who cares about each child, who teaches from the heart.

Dear Mim
Thank you for comeing
I was shy to dance
but you made me feel
better and I danced
Love,
Meredith

57

Good teaching must always be seen as "work in progress." Those who share the journey of educating children will find in Mimi's observations much to amuse, encourage, and inspire.

The First

30 Years

of Teaching

Are the Hardest:

Notes From the

Yellow Brick Road

I visited with Sister Miriam at an education conference. We are old conference friends. She is probably one of the last nuns in America to wear her old, traditional habit. And, she never dropped other old habits, such as lovingness, caring, playfulness, and sharing.

I whispered, "Sister Miriam, this is my 30th year of teaching!" She returned the confidence, "This is my 60th! The first 30 years are the hardest!" I planted a tree for her in Israel in honor of her 60th year of teaching.

* * *

A child asked, "How long have you been a teacher?"
"Thirty years," the teacher replied.
"Well," the child concluded, "you must know how to do it by heart."

* * *

These are notes from the heart as we journey along in search of Oz, Kansas, The Wizard, Courage, Brains, Heart. In search of . . .

I met a teacher I hadn't seen for many years. He asked if I was still teaching.
"Of course," I answered.
His eyes showed surprise.
"I'm going to keep trying until I get it right," I said.

These are notes from the journey as we bump along, losing and finding our way, stopping at scenic routes, detouring at danger spots, speeding along on cruise control, plunging into the traffic snarls. Notes from the heart. . . Notes from the start. . .

I started teaching young children on a stage in the gym of a shabby, overcrowded school in upstate New York in 1956. We had a teacher shortage in America then. We had few materials—no high-interest, low-vocabulary, shiny books. No colorful filmstrips, overhead projectors, opaques, video libraries, Apple computers. Just apples, the children, and us!

Since that time I've worked with toddlers to senior citizens, from Head Start to Upward Bound, from gifted and talented to learning disabled, from overachievers to underachievers, from ghettos to suburbs, from New York to Hawaii. The things I believed then, I believe now— only stronger. Today these beliefs are as solid as the House Made of Bricks (Yellow *Brick* Road? House Made of *Bricks*? Oh well, these are just *notes*.) My beliefs started out flimsy, easy to blow over, almost as fragile as the House Made of Straw. Time and children helped me to turn the straw into bricks, no wolf or wind can blow this house over. I believe in loving children, in loving people. I believe in caring, playfulness, sharing, courage. . .

All of my T-shirts are reading materials. Some of the messages printed on my shirts read:

"I am still learning." (Michelangelo's motto)

"Teaching is one of the few professions that permits love." (Roethke)

"The lesson that is not enjoyed is not learned." (Talmud)

I was driving to an AEYC conference in Canfield, Ohio. The directions Muriel Hampton sent me were excellent, clear as calligraphy. I followed them to the letter. I got lost— totally, dismally lost. I asked and followed, understood and misunderstood. I ended up in a phone booth outside of a restaurant and called Muriel.

"This is where I am. I don't know where it is. Please, come and meet me!" Muriel was astonished. "You're only a mile away. But, it's impossible for you to be at *that* restaurant if you followed my directions!"

We in education know the impossible is our everyday agenda. There are many ways to reach our destinations. Sometimes, the way prescribed is *not* the way that succeeds. We have our educational goals, our directives, our curriculum guidelines. Often, we are given preset ways to accomplish those goals. Sometimes those ways don't work. We mustn't think there is only *one* approach. But, if goals, approaches, and curriculum grow out of children's ages, stages, interests, and feelings, they are more *likely* to work. Even so, we mustn't think there *is* only one approach.

A Native American saying goes something like this: "Let all the paths recognize each other."

Recently, I worked with children in a city school under their Artists-in-the-Schools program. I walked into one of the rooms while the children were at recess. This gave me a few minutes to explore before they came back. The walls of this room were papered with *rules: If You Do This, That Will Happen to You; If You Dare to Do This Twice, These Things Will Be Your Punishment;* and so on.

Each item was very specific—sit in *this* position, line up in *that* location. The rules covered every waking moment, every behavior possibility. I expected the world's most obedient, cooperative, courteous children. Instead, I was almost trampled by rude, rough, mean-spirited children running, fighting, and shouting into the room. This group was one of the most difficult I have worked with. I was dismayed by the children's behavior.

After our session, I had a chance to spend a few minutes with their teacher, who frustratedly told me, "These are the toughest children I have taught in 10 years of teaching." I looked at her room of ignored rules and collective rudeness and responded honestly, from the gut, "If something isn't working, don't keep doing it."

We talked for a while. I shared my feelings. "These rules aren't working with *these* children. Every class is a special mix of specific individuals. Every year is a new year. Maybe nothing you have ever studied or learned will work with this particular group of children. You'll have to try everything—known and unknown— old and new, borrowed and blue, to find ways to reach them. What do they care about? What do they respond to? What touches them? What are their interests? When are they most responsive? What's on their magic vocabulary list? Who are their heroes?"

As I left, a child slipped me a note. It read: "Please don't leave us."

* * *

I still believe as I have always believed—there are no unreachable children, only those who are, as yet, unreached. That is a leap of faith. As we believe, so we teach. In my

House of Bricks a tapestry hangs. Sewn on the fabric is the Edwin Markham poem:

> He drew a circle that shut me out
> Heretic, rebel, a thing to flout.
> But *love* and I had the wit to win
> We drew a circle that took him in.

I think that poem is the core of what education is all about. The great teachers I know are circle drawers. They never accept being left out nor agree to leave a child out. They continuously make larger and larger circles to take in an alienated child, to turn a child from *off* to *on*, to help a child who knows only failure to taste success, to change the history of a child with a broken self-image. Never give up on a child! on children! Sometimes, you may be the *only* person who hasn't given up— even with a very young child. Sometimes, you are the only person making that leap of faith, the only person believing in that child.

* * *

Stop on the scenic route and spend time with teachers like Ronni Hochman Spratt who teaches special education. She's a shouter, a screamer, a laugher, a hugger, a lover, a friend, a taskmaster. No doubts about where she stands on the major issues of the day. She votes *life* all the way!

She tells children who have had numerous experiences with failure, "You are *not* going to fail in my class. Even if you try, I won't let you! Do you hear me? I won't permit it! You are going to succeed (or else)." She cajoles, threatens, rewards, jokes, tickles, celebrates. Her children succeed. All education should be *special!*

Another idea written on the walls of my House Made of Bricks is the Yiddish proverb, "All of my children are prodigies."

If you believe it and live it every day, you'll find that it's true. I have never had a child who did not demonstrate originality, creativity, imagination, surprising talents. The children are all there waiting for us to believe in them, to expect the *best* from them. In this high-tech, high-anxiety, computer-crazed, supercharged age, children need us to hallow them more than ever. Through it all, do you have the courage?

* * *

I did a workshop with education majors who were involved in their teaching practicums. They were sharing projects. One team reported on an outstanding zoo project that took weeks of writing, reading, researching, math, art, science—all the curriculum strands interwoven (as all good education weaves). One of the subtopics was a listing of endangered species that the eight-year-old children had researched. The university student–teachers read off the list. I felt my hand raised and heard myself say, "There's an endangered species you forgot—*the spirits of children.*"

I'm worried about our children. In our pressured-hurry-up system, many of them are learning earlier than ever to be failures, to lose faith in themselves, to feel inhibited, squelched, defeated, discouraged, closed off, anxious, apathetic.

Frayda Turkel and Miriam Flock Schulman, dance teachers in an Artists-in-the-Schools program, shared music and dance with children in a school for the physically disabled. In keeping with inclusive goals, a class of nondisabled children came to the program with their teacher, who turned out to be a very uptight, stern, joyless person. Miriam and Frayda drummed, chanted, talked, and sang. They invited the children to join them. From all corners of the gym, children in wheelchairs, on crutches, in braces limped, rolled, hobbled, or crawled forward eagerly to participate. Only the nondisabled children, frozen in their seats by their teacher's strict stare, never moved. Which children had the real limitations?

The director of a preschool and her staff took a day off to visit another program in the city. They observed young children learning in silence with minimal interaction, passive lessons, formal instruction, and ditto sheets galore. When the children went to the restroom, they walked in single file with their hands on top of their heads. Talking wasn't allowed.

That night, my friend watched a television program about prisoners of war. She gasped as she watched the prisoners walk single file, hands on top of their heads. Talking wasn't allowed.

Today, we still have classrooms of harsh silence and of fear. The spirits of our children are endangered.

* * *

I want to launch a nationwide anti-smug campaign. I am meeting more and more children who already know everything!

"We already studied colors!"

"We had the human body in second grade!"

"We did nutrition last year!" (I told them about the scientist Dr. McClintock who has been studying kernels of corn on the cob for 60 years and she hasn't finished corn yet.)

I asked a group of children if they had followed the historic reappearance of Halley's comet. They answered, "We finished the solar system." I'm worried about the shrinking of minds, the closing of doors and windows, the shriveling of curiosity and wonder.

As I believe, so I teach. Educators and parents, join the anti-smug campaign! Down with convergent thinking and closed, absolute right-and-wrong answers! Up with divergent thinking and open-ended, exploring, brainstorming, wonder-full discussions and questions!

Let's preserve the minds and spirits of our children and ourselves as fiercely as we fight to preserve endangered species like baby seals and whales. My notes read—*Trust your instincts.*

"The greatest technique in the universe is the technique in the human heart." (Margolit Ovid)

* * *

I visited Brenda's Sim's class of young authors. Her children were in a group hug, Brenda in the middle. She beamed as she announced, "Mimi, these are the most talented, creative, delightful writers. Every one of them is imaginative and original. Now, Charles sometimes has to have his work translated from the original. . . ."

Charles grinned and showed me one of his original papers. Totally indecipherable. Any but a life-affirming, loving teacher might have tossed it into the nearest wastepaper basket along with a barrage of scolding. But, Brenda found a technique to help Charles succeed and improve without losing faith in himself. When he proudly shared his

rewritten paper— clearer and neater at the bottom of the page he had signed, "Translated from the original by Charles."

Dawn Heyman is another teacher who has a love affair with teaching and her children. They come from the inner-city and single-parent homes where English is a second language. Her children come to school when they're sick. They don't want to miss a minute. In some other classes, children come to school well and *get* sick.

One of Dawn's students asked her, "Do you know what my four favorite things in the world are?" Dawn couldn't guess.

"Number one is school. Number two is school. Number three is school. Number four is school."

When Mary Sue Garlinger, a movement educator, visited a class for a day, she later received a letter from one of the children. "Thank you for coming today. You made me happy for the rest of my life."

In my House Made of Bricks, in my journey on the Yellow Brick Road, I've come more and more to the conclusion that there are only two choices in education: life and death! If you are undecided, indifferent, neutral, apathetic, you are on the side of *death*—death of ideas, of excitement, of discovery. Death of the spirit.

If you are on the side of *life*, you can't go wrong. Oh, you can make mistakes, lose your way, misunderstand your goals, misinterpret directions, but you can't go wrong with children who know you love them and are committed to their welfare, to their minds, to their healthy growth— dedicated to the sacredness of your precious time together.

Rhoda Linder took her preschoolers for a field trip and got lost. They wandered around for a while looking for the right place. Rhoda was flustered and embarrassed. When they finally found their destination, four-year-old Peter beamed his shining smile up at her and burst, "We're very proud of you."

* * *

There are more notes than space, more notes than time to write them all. There are so many life-filled teachers, principals, parents, child care workers, and children on the journey—walking with us, lighting our way, enriching the trip—that I could fill a book with their names alone.

I am lucky to know them and feel their warmth. In our field of education, sometimes our lights dim and get buried beneath a bombardment of instructional strategies, methods, and materials.

Sister Miriam, I'm at the 30-year mark! I see you ahead, rainbow bright and glistening. As early childhood educators—*as human beings*—we are all on the Yellow Brick Road seeking Courage, Brains, and Heart. Like Dorothy, Tin Man, Scarecrow, and Lion, we already have these gifts, but we don't always know it. We forget a lot. In spite of pressures to the contrary, we need to dig out our courage to teach in ways that are loyal to the spirits of young children.

I agree with the Tin Woodsman who said, "Brains are not the best thing in the world. Once I had brains and a heart also; having tried them both, I would much rather have a heart."

These are notes from the heart.

"What Has Two Legs and Loves You?"

Some years ago, I was the keynote presenter for a nearby city school system's in-service day. On the night before the program, knowing that my vocabulary is somewhat unconstrained, one of the teachers from that district called with a warning that the superintendent was "very very strict, Mimi." "He's so straight," she said, "that he won't even permit the use of the expression *four-letter words*, never mind any specific four-letter words themselves, so *be careful* tomorrow!"

I thanked her for her advice and immediately began gathering all the four-letter words that came to mind. The list passed one hundred without my referring to the dictionary.

The next day, facing the crowded auditorium, I started my address by saying, "Today, let's devote ourselves to considering a group of four-letter words." At the mere mention of the forbidden expression, a gasp rose from the audience. All eyes turned toward the superintendent who himself turned a pale green color.

I continued, "I recommend that we paper our walls with these words, turn them into credit cards, write them in the sky! These are some four-letter words that creative, caring educators should have on their lips and in their hearts at all times!" Another audible gasp from the group.

I read them my one hundred words. Here is just a small sampling from that list. (Add your own to make your own hundred!)

Grow	Seek	Seed	Near
Open	Life	Rich	Fair
Warm	Live	Song	Calm
Safe	Lift	Hope	Laud
Free	Care	Poem	Plan
Give	Rise	Need	Help
Show	Vary	Risk	Zany
Sing	Play	Dare	Idea
Grin	Wide	Link	Know
Bend	Hear	Find	Good

The audience cheered with relief! The best four-letter word I saved for last and first and always: *love*.

Theodore Roethke's belief that teaching is one of the few professions that permits love is demonstrated every minute of every day in classrooms and schools throughout the country by educators who truly *care* about their students.

At workshops I remind teachers and administrators that

> You *may be the only person who sees, listens to, thinks about, believes in this child. Many of our children are lonely and deprived of attention. Many of our children feel alienated, disconnected. There are many more children missing in America than those featured on airport posters or milk cartons. Some of our missing kids sit before us each day— untapped, untouched, unknown.* You *may not even realize that your basic warmth and interest may be sustaining the life and spirit of a child.* You *may not even realize that you make the difference between life and death of self-image, of confidence, of feelings of well-being and self-worth in the lives of your children.*

This urgent reminder is dramatized in a most moving way by Don Bartlette, who shares his story with educators around the country—the story of a very poor, physically and emotionally handicapped Native American child who faced daily neglect, deprivation, and humiliation from family, classmates, and *teachers* for most of his childhood and young adulthood. He tells of the miracle of one woman in the community who reached out to him—believing in him, teaching him to talk, to eat, to learn, to believe in himself. Don Bartlette said, "All I ever wanted was what every child wants, someone to walk along with me." (Teaching is one of the few professions that permits love.)

How do we show this love? In *everything* we do—in the way we talk and greet, listen and respond, mediate and teach, explain and scold, include and exclude, grin and grimace. In the safe climate we create—the healthy, life-affirming learning place that is our space. We demonstrate our love in big and small ways. Sometimes, in ways so imperceptible that most observers will not even catch the event.

Robin Covel Moel, an art teacher, was standing with a colleague when Jerry, a high school special education student, rushed to them with an exciting plan. He wanted to make a macramé necklace for his friend.

Robin's colleague shook her head, "No, he's in special ed; macramé is too hard." Just as Jerry was sinking, Robin winked at him and saved him from drowning again (lots of our kids drown every day). She said, "Where there's a will, there's a way. Let's give it a try."

Jerry's lucky friend wears her macramé necklace today with pride! (Don't tell the person who's doing something that he can't do it!) Loving teachers say, "We'll find a way."

How do we show this love? In the way we believe in the children. Their lives, experiences, knowledge, and interests are valid. Their ideas are needed to fuel the energy of the classroom. Each child is needed for the success and happiness of the group. The class is a tight, close, caring group of sharing people—learning together, helping each other, enjoying the excitement of the educational process and the time together. Special time. Sacred time. All education should be special!

How do we show this love? In the fierce ways that put-downs, meanness, teasing, and humiliation are outlawed in our rooms, in our schools. In our space, people are safe! The way we learn is affected by the way we live in the learning environment. If we live in anxiety and fear, our learning possibilities shrivel. Fairness and consistency in our own behavior are a new language for many children who are gifted and talented in bullying others and in putting themselves down. If we're stubborn, strong in our beliefs, gutsy, aware, and sensitive, change *will* take place. In our rooms, in our schools, we celebrate positive behavior, downplay negative behavior. That's the way it is in our place!

What happens when we show our love? The returns are astonishing. Younger children shower us with affection and devotion. Older, more inhibited boys and girls show it to us in more subtle ways.

One of my favorite hobbies is saving love stories of teachers and children and administrators. My collection could fill volumes. Here are a few examples.

After a few weeks off for personal leave, Maureen Reedy returned to her class. When the children came in and saw her sitting at her desk, they were ecstatic. One of the girls flung her arms around Maureen, shouting joyfully, "Miss Reedy is back and now all my problems are over!"

In another elementary school, Tom Griffin's class presented him with a surprise book at the end of the year chronicling the highlights of the year. The kids were overwhelming in their specific praises of Tom.

"You are a great teacher. You teach us a new and fun way of learning. Even though I lost my papers, I still liked it. . . ." (Jenny)

"You have influenced my thoughts and the way I look at things. . . . Your literature program has been new, exciting, and great. I think this year has had me learn more than at any other grade in school. . . ." (Jennifer)

"Thank you for being my teacher this year. I really learned a lot. I learned how to read faster and how to write a review. I also learned how to do many things with numbers. I am learning how weather happens and how electricity is produced. I also had a lot of fun, making pillows and Jane Yolen Day. I have a real lot of fun when you sing to us on Friday at the end of the day. I had a real good year and I hope you did, too." (Chris)

"You are a great teacher. You have many different ways of teaching. You have taught all of us so many things. You let us tell you our opinion on certain things and you always have something to say about it. You give us confidence in lots of things. I like morning

meetings because you find out what's happening
around the world. I think you do everything to help us.
You make school lots of fun for everybody." (Carrie)

"Mr. Griffin, thanks!
   You made us feel like family with your guitar and
      singing!

Mr. Griffin, thanks!
   I was scared at first because you were my first male
      teacher.
   But, you were kind and understanding to us.

Mr. Griffin, thanks!
   You taught us to say what we feel. Through the bad
      times and good times you were always there.

Mr. Griffin, thanks!
   We were not always a group.
   You helped us.
   So, thanks!" (Megan)

* * *

At the end of a busy, harried day, Dawn Heyman looked
up to see one of her smallest, most stuttery second graders
coming eagerly to her with a riddle.
   "M-M-Miss Heyman, what has two l-l-legs and l-l-loves
you?" Dawn thought for a while, then gave up. Eugene's
smile was as bright as noon. "M-m-m-Me!"
   (*All I ever wanted was what every child wants—someone to
walk along with me.—Don Bartlette*)

* * *

Actually, I agree with our nervous superintendent. Four-
letter words can be very dangerous. Why, words like *love*
could spread from class to class and, before you know it, in
the hands of loving administrators and teachers could affect
an entire school!
   Kelly Stevens, a dynamic, fun-filled, fanatically devoted
principal believes school is a family, community, inter-
generational affair. During the school year, she asked
children and families to let her know how they thought
school was going. An avalanche of technicolored heart-
shaped answers poured into her office. Enjoy these few
examples of the answers she received:
   "We care and share in our children's education . . . it's like
belonging to one big family and everyone wants to help. . . ."
   "Teachers care. . . . Our school is safe. . . ."
   "My son is being taught the knowledge that will help him
in his adult world . . . warm and wonderful teachers mold
lives. . . ."
   "Someone takes time to listen. . . . All will hear and see
us. . . ."
   "Teachers show concern for each of their students. . . ."
   "The principal treats us like part of her family. . . ."
   "Special people treat children as worthwhile individuals. . . ."
   "The teachers are intelligent, tremendous, helpful, fun to
be with, and they care about us. . . ."
   "We love the friendships we've made here. . . .We love all
the people who work here. . . ."
   "The teachers really care about our children. . . ."
All those four-letter words fell on Kelly's school like confetti!

Let's move from one school to a whole school system. When loving, caring, committed educators plan enrichment activities for whole districts, they are fired with enthusiasm in anticipation of meaningful experiences their students will enjoy. As Diane Oliver explained some of her plans for her district for the coming year, she counted the days until school began. "I can't wait till the children come back!"

Now, speaking of four-letter words, let's start out with *love*. Where do we go from there?

Dear Mimi

Thank you I for words. now I can write very long storys.

Your freind,
Johanna

Every teacher has had a child who remains outside the group, giving little sign of interest or involvement in what's going on. To bring that child into the group—not by force, but by patience, caring, and ingenuity—is the challenge.

We Drew a Circle That Took Him In

Randy is in your class. See him with the half-closed eyes and slumpy back leaning against the wall when everyone's jumping with the excitement of an idea? Why is his head on the table while other eyes are beaming their brights on you? Randy doesn't respond when you ask a question or seem to be listening when you read a story. *What to do about Randy?*

Through all these long school years, through all the Randys, I agonized over these questions: Where did we go wrong? How can these children be reached? What can we do to connect with them? The Randys who behaved as "disturbed," in addition to tuned out or turned off, were referred to trained psychologists or counselors. But the majority of the Randys weren't in need of professional treatment. They were under the headings of "indifferent" or "nonparticipating."

Through all these long school years, through all these Randys, I have threatened, pleaded, bribed, nudged, cajoled, whimpered, and begged. None of those approaches succeeded in changing catatonic-looking Randys into healthy, involved, active children. But, as many of us do, I adhered to that age-old practice: If it doesn't work, keep doing it! For years, I kept doing it and it hadn't worked, so finally I decided to look at the Randys with a different perspective. I changed my head! I turned on my windshield wipers. I had clearer vision.

The experience of my friend Candace Mazur, who works with Artists-in-the-Schools, reminded me of something I already knew but had forgotten. She saw a nonparticipating Randy standing apart, semi-watching her imaginative troll celebrations with a large group of children. She glanced at that Randy but had no time to do anything special to catch him in her web of enchantment. She thought to herself, can't win them all, and turned her attention back to the group.

That night at the school open house, a couple came toward her, gushing with enthusiasm. "Whatever you did today, Candace, you really turned our son on! Why, that boy came home from school, ran to his room, and changed it into a troll's den!" You guessed it. The couple were Randy's parents!

Over the years, I had forgotten that most of our non-participating Randys who are half-listening, their flags at half-mast, are really with us. They go home and report on "what we did today." In many cases, parents never know that their children have not demonstrated one gesture of interest.

Contributing to my newly discovered insight is a strong new approach. It's based on the following beliefs and it works!

There is no way any child can be left out of anything we do!

There is no way any child can leave himself or herself out of anything we do!

Even if our Randys are as stiff as lava-stoned Pompeii figures or as turned off as power failures, in my mind, these children are with us. Our circle takes them in. Here's some of the vocabulary that reflects this *way* of teaching—teaching in "the key of life":

"We need someone to watch the parade. Thanks, Randy. . . ."

"Oh, who will be the audience for our circus? Randy, thanks for volunteering!"

"We need someone waiting for the group to come home from the zoo. Randy, will you be the person waiting? Thanks a lot!"

"Randy, will you be the person standing at the corner waiting for the traffic to pass? Thanks!"

Now, after a while, Randy is bombarded with participation suggestions. Mind you, he hasn't moved one muscle! He hasn't even agreed to the offers. But, because my blood type is B-positive, I believe that he is always participating, appreciated, and needed.

Let me tell you about our latest Randy. This Randy has not budged in my movement sessions with his kindergarten class since September. But, he's never left out. (See above examples.) I must confess, however, that over these months I have lost it and resorted sometimes to kidding. "Randy, don't overdo it! Don't strain yourself!" Once in a while, I've tricked him into a trace of a smile.

This has gone on for three seasons. Now we're into spring and today I am waiting for Randy's class. His teacher wants us to enrich our study of nutrition. I am ready with a curriculum.

The kindergartners bounce in. My eyes blink. Am I seeing things? Is that Randy bouncing in with the others? I am in shock. Randy is dancing over to me. Randy is excited. Randy bursts with the news!

"Mimi! I can snap!"

Randy's hand is in the air. Randy's fingers snap, crackle, pop. Castanet fingers. Randy is proud. He can't stop snapping. This calls for immediate response. A superstructured teacher might say:

"That's nice, Randy. But, we're not scheduled for snapping until the third week in May. Can you hold your snap?" or "Randy, this isn't sharing time. Why not wait till next Tuesday's sharing time to show us your snap" or "Snapping is interesting, Randy, but today we are studying nutrition, so snap out of it!"

But, as you know, creative teachers improvise and invent a lot. Here's what happened. I said, "Randy! This is amazing! Are you a mind reader? How did you know that we're doing a story today that desperately *needs* snapping?"

Randy is hopping with excitement.

Here's the story I instantly made up. We did it with movement (of course) and drama (of course) and music (of course) and language skills (of course) and followed with pictures and words (of course).

"Those of you who can snap, get ready. Those who can't, fake it."

We snapped fingers.

"Once upon a time it was raining (snap). Thundering (we boomed)! Lightning (we jabbed)! Far from their homes, rabbits were playing. Oh, no! Rain! The rabbits hopped quickly back to their rabbit hutches."

I turned on bouncy music. We all hopped back to our shelter.

Randy, the hopping rabbit, moved with his rabbit friends as if he had been moving with them since birth. (Naturally, we always move in the same direction around the room. Safety first!)

"The rabbits reached their shelter. They shook off the rain. They talked in rabbit language translated into English. What do you think they said?"

"I got rain in my ears." (Gretchen)

"My tail is all wet." (Jeremy)

"I hopped in a puddle." (Melissa)

Well, you get the idea. Oooops! The teacher is glaring at me. What happened to *nutrition?* Not to worry!

"Well, now the rabbits are ready to sleep. What nutritious snack can they have before bedtime?"

"Carrots!" (Jordan)

"Lettuce!" (Mitchell)

You get the idea, dear reader, and so the story continued. The rain kept falling in finger snaps. The thunder and lightning kept thundering and lightning, booming and jabbing. Far from their homes, horses, birds, deer, and children had to gallop, fly, leap, and jog. Of course, when each of these animals and humans reached home and dried off, they had nutritious snacks. What nutritious snacks can *you* think of? Well, you get the idea!

The whole session took 15 minutes—from the class bouncing in, to Randy's snappy announcement, to the story with at least five separate chapters, to the summary of nutritious snacks.

As miraculously as a snake sheds its skin, as Leo the Late Bloomer blooms, Randy the Snapper charged into life. Because, in our time together, Randy has always participated ("Thanks for being the person who isn't paying attention, Randy!"), we couldn't express our monumental astonishment and joy! Because we never let his circles leave us out and always drew circles that took him in, then when he really jumped in, it was just a lovely, everyday event—no big thing.

In my notebook I scribbled, "From Catatonic to Hyperactive: Randy Snapped Today." No big thing? Then why, after school that day, did the kindergarten teachers and I laugh and cry?

Words of

Encouragement:

Honey on the Page

Lisa is ten. We are driving together on a Saturday afternoon and talking about the wonderful computer in her classroom.

"It can do everything! It has so much power! It's so much fun!" She loves that computer.

I am honest about my feelings. I tell her that I believe in the power of good teachers, not machines. Do computers have laps? Can computers hug? Do computers have shoulders to cry on? When do computers surprise us with spontaneous, unsolicited ideas?

I ask Lisa, "Which would you rather have? An interesting, challenging, exciting teacher or your computer?" She answers without hesitation, "I'd rather have my computer than my teacher."

I am stunned. "Why?"

"Well, the computer is . . . " she searches for words, the right word, "the computer is warm."

"WARM?" I am shouting.

"Yeah, the computer is warm and my teacher is . . . " she narrows her eyes and adds, "*cold.*"

I am speechless.

"The computer," she continues, "is—*comforting*. It's *encouraging*. If you make a mistake, it says, 'Try again' or 'Better luck next time.' If you get it right, it says, 'Good job' or 'Fine job!' My teacher never tells us we did well. She's never satisfied. We're never good enough for her. She never gives us words of praise. No matter how great you do, she never tells you she's pleased."

As we drive along, I admit to myself that given the choice between a machine programmed to be comforting, warm, and encouraging and a teacher who programs herself to be negative, discouraging, and cold, I, too, would choose the machine!

Lisa's confession haunts me. At home, I walk our dogs and meet almost-three-year-old Tia at the peak of celebrating her very first success at skipping. We cheer for her. "Yaaaaay! Right on! Super Skipper!" We applaud, smile, hug. Tia skips down the driveway, eyes shining with pride and accomplishment. I remember back to Tia's major steps: her first walking, her first talking, and now her first skipping. Each stage was accompanied by the affectionate encouragement and praise from family and friends.

When does the celebrating of learning stop?

Lisa's feelings about the warmth of her computer and the cold of her teacher continue to obsess me. I think about seven-year-old Andrew who rushed excitedly into his house one day after school.

"Mom," he called, "We have a new teacher—the *best*, the very *best* teacher I ever had!"

"But I thought you liked your other teacher," Andrew's mother wondered.

"I do, but our new teacher is the *best*. Our other teacher said, 'No, No, No' and our new teacher says '*Yes! Yes! Yes!*'"

Language is the core, the key, the foundation of every class, subject, activity, and relationship. We should say *languages*: the language of the textbooks, printed materials, curriculum resources; the language of daily events—the give and take, instructions, directions, announcements, reactions, questions, and conversations; the language of feelings—the life and death of the spirit conveyed through verbal and nonverbal communication; the power of the teacher's language helping children learn and grow together or the flip-side when the teacher's language conveys negatives to children—You're dumb! Look at those mistakes! This work isn't good. This is language of the shrinking of the spirit.

Are you a *yes* teacher or a *no* teacher? A vote for *life*—for *yes*—yields immeasurable rewards. A vote for *no* has dire implications. Read on!

The first graders were instructed to make a clock and be sure that all the numbers for the hours were written clearly. Katy jumped into the assignment with enthusiasm. She carefully wrote the 12 numbers of the clock on a round paper plate. They were perfect and so beautiful that she was inspired to decorate each number with a tiny flower around it. She hurried to school with her colorful clock held in her hands like an offering.

A different child returned home from school that day. Back slumped, head bent, eyes down, she opened the door.

"Did your teacher like your clock, Katy?" her mother asked anxiously.

Without a word, Katy dropped the clock on the floor. Her mother picked it up. Across the face of the clock, scratched so deeply it tore the paper, was a huge X and in angry handwriting, the teacher's message: "Did not follow instructions!"

When does the celebrating of learning stop?

There is an old Yiddish custom. When young children completed a page of study, their teacher dropped a dot of honey on the bottom of the page. The children were encouraged to dip their finger in the honey and taste its sweetness. Learning should always be sweet!

I shared this custom with teachers at a workshop. One of the participants couldn't contain herself and related this story. That very week, her own first grader brought home a paper. There on the top of Jeff's paper, his teacher had pasted a Sad Face with tear drops flowing from the eyes and down the entire length of the paper. At the bottom, next to the stream of tears, was clearly printed: "I am very disappointed in your work."

When Lisa, Tia, Andrew, Katy, Johnny, and Jeff come to your class, what will they find? Who will they find?

Will they find a teacher who is "user friendly"?

Will they find a teacher programmed to be comforting, warm, and encouraging?

Will the language of the classroom be *Yes?*

Will you spin words of praise, drop honey on the page, and say in everything you do—"The celebrating of learning never stops"?

Say *Yes!*

Fortunate are the children who spend time with one of those loving educators who see what each child is capable of doing and never give up on anyone. Together they are gathered in "that starlit field where teachers shine."

"That Starlit Field Where Teachers Shine"

I always look forward to Sister Iona Taylor's annual newsletter. Full of lively updates on her travels, friends, causes, and insights, each page radiates Iona's spirit.

Iona is one of those folks who just don't get it! Instead of retiring, she rejuvenates. From classroom teacher to administrator to consultant to "doctor of education" who makes home visits in her over 50 years of life work in the field of education, she has journeyed the world with reading programs and projects. When she reached retirement age, she turned down an invitation to return to the Mother House of her religious order and chose to join Grace Pilon, the creator of Workshop Way at Xavier University in New Orleans. After six years at Xavier, Sister Iona graciously declined another invitation from her Mother House to enjoy a well-deserved rest. Instead, she moved into a trailer, visited shut-ins, taught children, gave Holy Communion, and helped take the census—in ministerial work for her parish in the Bayou country of Louisiana.

Now, where is Sister Iona? Her newsletter reports that she is in Ohio caring for an older woman, participating in the life of the community and, of course, teaching—now first grade Sunday School.

She writes: "My first graders are challenging. They are very alert and keep me in that starlit field where teachers shine."

Funny about Iona! She always makes me think. As I fold her newsletter, I picture Amy, a young teacher working and playing with children with special needs. Proudly showing photos of the children in her class, most of whom are challenged by profound disabilities, she sparkles as she shares:

"He's so funny! He has us laughing all day! What a sense of humor!"

"She's the sweetest girl. So creative. . . . "

"This child asks the most wonderful questions."

Later, when I tell Amy, "Your children are so lucky to have you for a teacher," without hesitation, she responds, "No, Mim, I'm privileged to have *them*."

Amy and all of you in the family of loving educators who see into the hearts of children, who find the *able* in the word dis*able*, who know that the *real* handicapped are those handicapped in spirit—you are journeying with Iona in that "starlit field."

* * *

"Take my advice, Pat," the troublemaker's third grade teacher warned. "That one is impossible. Let him know that one more misbehavior from him and he's *out*."

Pat pretended ignorance. She gave the child the opportunity to begin again and again, and because she gave him a million chances and taught him the repetition of trust and faith, he responded. Over the months the boy's communication and behavior grew more positive. Pat was relentless in seeing him as a valued person with important ideas and opinions, with contributions to make.

Pat and all of you in the family of loving educators who refuse to label, stamp, categorize, and prejudge children; who are willing to offer them opportunities to share their gifts; who let them know that you believe in them and expect the best from them; who inspire fairness by demonstrating fairness; who teach respect by showing respect—you are walking with Iona in "that starlit field where teachers shine."

Oh, Iona, that field is filled with teachers! They will be difficult to interview. They are too busy encouraging, prodding, preparing, listening, comforting, exploring, joking, talking, laughing, gathering, guiding, watching, discovering, singing, reading, planning, showing, and caring. That field, Iona, is buzzing with words like *hands-on, whole language, collaborative, cooperative, interactive, developmentally appropriate, multicultural, relevant, self-affirming, multifaceted*. Every word positive and pulsing with *life*.

Iona, your first grade Sunday School kids have certainly discovered by now that their teacher is an adventurer, constantly challenging and exciting their minds.

Because of you. Because of the children.

Because of you and the children.

Because you are full of faith in the children and in the sacredness of learning together, you are gathered in that "starlit field," never burning out, always shining.

And we are with you on the field trip.

Josh

Rachel

Chris S.

Mimi's Promices

1. we would run out of time
2. we would use our powers
3. we would get thirsty.
4. we would have fun.

The many images of "teaching in the key of life" offered in this volume will incite many teachers to infuse their own classrooms with greater joy, creativity, and movement. For those who are eager to read further, here are

More Resources for Teaching in the Key of Life

From Mimi's Bookshelf

My bookshelves burst with inspiring, stimulating materials. They are uncategorized, disorganized. I love my books, add to them, never replace them—they just multiply as the shelves heave from their weight. A few of my favorites follow in the hopes that some of these books will vie for a place on *your* list of favorites and that your collection of books will soon push against your bookends.

—Mimi

Ashton-Warner, S. (1963). *Teacher.* New York: Simon & Shuster.

This grand old book includes a rich account of using children's own words for teaching beginning reading. Full of truth, wisdom, and inspiration.

Calkins, L.M. (1985). *Lessons from a child: The teaching and learning of writing.* Portsmouth, NH: Heinemann.

I love this book because on every page is stamped respect and admiration for the minds and spirits of children.

Canner, N. (1975). *And a time to dance: A sensitive exposition of the use of creative movement with retarded children* (2nd ed.). Boston: Plays Inc.

Every page of this practical book about dancing with young children is infused with a love of children and of dance—a natural combination.

Dewey, J. (1979). *Experience and education* (Collier 21st ed.). New York: Macmillan.

To offset our smugness, we must remember that our great thinkers like John Dewey articulated decades ago a conception of children's learning and education that lies at the heart of "developmentally appropriate practice." Many people still don't "get it!"

Edelman, M.W. (1992). *The measure of our success: A letter to my children and yours.* New York: HarperCollins.

I am such an admirer of M.W. Edelman, her life and her work. This little book has much wisdom in it and reflects her beautiful spirit and strength.

Greenberg, P. (1990). *The devil has slippery shoes: A biased biography of the Child Development Group of Mississippi (CDGM)—A story of maximum feasible poor parent participation.* Washington, DC: Youth Policy Institute.

This book tells the powerful story of thousands of African American Mississippians in the sixties who struggled together to improve the education of their children through organizing and operating a statewide network of Head Start centers. It's exhilarating and immensely moving.

Holt, J. (1970). *What do I do Monday?* New York: Dutton.

I like everything about John Holt's philosophy, especially his theory of the "four worlds." Check it out.

Hopkins, S., & Winters, J. (Eds.). (1990). *Discover the world: Empowering children to value themselves, others and the earth.* Philadelphia: New Society.

This is not a poetic book but a practical workbook. Why do I like it? I love the subtitle. I think that the themes themselves, such as "Concerns of Peace" and "Appreciation of the Environment," direct our awareness, and the specific suggestions are excellent.

Kohl, H. (1967). *36 Children.* New York: New American Library.

I first read this book in 1968 on a train from Albany to New York City to present some workshops. I cried all the way down from Albany. Every person who cares about kids should read this book. I still cry.

Lopate, P. (1973). *Being with children.* New York: Doubleday.

This is another of those books that make you rededicate yourself to children. I love Lopate's term, "noodling around" with the kids. I added that expression to my "messin' around," "kibbitzin' around," and "hangin' out" with children! We're all in it together!

Moorman, C., & Moorman, N. (1989). *Teacher talk: What it really means.* Bay City, MI: Institute for Personal Power.

Chick and Nancy Moorman help every reader become aware of the effect our words have on children—our choice of expressions and questions. This is the kind of book that makes a difference in how we *are* with children.

Moorman, C., & Dishon, D. (1983). *Our classroom: We can learn together.* Englewood Cliffs, NJ: Prentice Hall.

Dee Dishon and Chick Moorman wrote this when the term "cooperative learning" was relatively new in the country. It is packed with wonderful, immediately usable, and important ideas that create a spirit of cooperation and cohesiveness.

Moyers, B., & Campbell, J. (1988). *The power of myth.* New York: Doubleday.

Joseph Campbell and Bill Moyers joined their talents to produce an unforgettable series of TV programs devoted to the power of myth. This book features an extended interview with Campbell, who has to be one of our most treasured resources. He takes you by the hand and pulls you into the drama, the excitement, the poetry of the myths and legends reflecting the imagination of the human family.

Neihardt, J. (1959). *Black Elk speaks.* New York: Simon & Schuster.

The wisdom of the Oglala Sioux (Lakota) Elder, as told to Neihardt in 1930, is simply mesmerizing. Black Elk's life, dreams, visions, and beliefs have so many important messages for us as we try to connect ourselves and our students to the environment, to nature, to each other.

Smilansky, S., Hagan, J., & Lewis, H. (1988). *Clay in the classroom.* New York: Teachers College Press.

In this practical study written in straight, informational chapters, the importance of children's learning through involvement, through hands-on interaction with materials is reinforced. Anyone who thinks children learn best through passive, rote, superstructured, teacher-directed approaches should be with children as they play with clay. A good reminder.

Welty, E. (1984). *One writer's beginnings.* Cambridge, MA: Harvard University Press.

Beautiful memoir of one of our outstanding writers. I especially love her memories as a very young child of listening to stories and listening *for* stories.

Yolen, J. (1981). *Touch magic. Fantasy, faerie and folklore in the literature of childhood.* New York: Philomel.

Jane Yolen's work is magic! Every page in this important little book pays tribute to the value of enchanting education. We must pass on to our children a legacy of imagination and language. Authentic learning goes way beyond information acquisition.

Further Readings

As Mimi asserts so emphatically, learning to teach well is a lifelong journey. Here are more resources to help educators in that journey.

The importance of play, the competence of children and other core ideas that underlie teaching in the key of life

Bredekamp, S., & Rosegrant, T. (Eds.). (1992). *Reaching potentials: Appropriate curriculum and assessment for young children* (Vol. 1). Washington, DC: NAEYC.

Christie, J.F., & Wardle, F. (1992). How much time is needed for play? *Young Children, 47*(3), 28–32.

Edwards, C., Gandini, L, & Forman, G. (1993). *The hundred languages of children: The Reggio Emilia approach to early childhood education.* Norwood, NJ: Ablex.

Katz, L.G. (1990). Impressions of Reggio Emilia preschools. *Young Children, 45*(6), 11–12.

New, R. (1990). Excellent early education: A city in Italy has it. *Young Children, 45*(6), 4–10.

More ideas for movement and dance, the visual arts, language and emerging literacy, and other things children love to do

Andress, B. (1991). Research in review. From research to practice: Preschool children and their movement responses to music. *Young Children, 47*(1), 22–27.

Andrews, P. (1976). Music and motion: The rhythmic language of children. *Young Children, 32*(1), 33–36.

Bohning, G., & Radencich, M. (1989). Action books. Pages for learning and laughter. *Young Children, 44*(6), 62–66.

Brown, T.M., & Laminack, L.L. (1989). Let's talk a poem. *Young Children, 44*(6), 49–52.

Chenfeld, M.B. (1987) *Teaching language arts creatively* (2nd. ed.) San Diego, CA: Harcourt Brace.

Chenfeld, M.B. (in press). *Creative experiences for young children* (2nd ed.). Ft. Worth, TX: Harcourt Brace.

Curtis, S. (1982). *The joy of movement in early childhood.* New York: Teachers College Press.

Dighe, J. (1993). Children and the earth. *Young Children, 48*(3), 58–63.

Feeney, S., & Moravcik, E. (1987). A thing of beauty: Aesthetic development in young children. *Young Children, 42*(6), 6–15.

Genishi, C. (1988). Research in review. Children's language: Learning words from experience. *Young Children, 44*(1), 16–23.

Gronlund, G. (1992). Coping with Ninja turtle play in my kindergarten classroom. *Young Children, 48*(1), 21–25.

Haiman, P.E. (1991). Viewpoint. Developing a sense of wonder in young children: There is more to early childhood education than cognitive development. *Young Children, 46*(6), 52–53.

Hayes, L.F. (1990). From scribbling to writing: Smoothing the way. *Young Children, 45*(3), 62–68.

Hill, D.M. (1977). *Mud, sand, and water.* Washington, DC: NAEYC.

Hitz, R. (1987). Creative problem solving through music activities. *Young Children, 42*(2), 12–17.

Hofschield, K.A. (1991). The gift of a butterfly. *Young Children, 46*(3), 3–6.

Honig, A.S. (1988). Research in review. Humor development in children. *Young Children, 43*(4), 60–73.

Howarth, M. (1989). Rediscovering the power of fairy tales. They help children understand their lives. *Young Children, 45*(1), 58–65.

Ishee, N., & Goldhaber, J. (1990). Story re-enactment: Let the play begin! *Young Children, 45*(3), 70–75.

Julius, A.K. (1979). Focus on movement: Practice and theory. *Young Children, 34*(1), 19–26.

Klein, A. (1991). All about ants: Discovery learning in the primary grades. *Young Children, 46*(5), 23–27.

McDonald, D.T. (1979). *Music in our lives: The early years.* Washington, DC: NAEYC.

NAEYC. (1988). Ideas that work with young children. Laughing all the way. *Young Children, 43*(2), 39–41.

Nunnelley, J.C. (1990). Beyond turkeys, santas, snowmen, and hearts: How to plan innovative curriculum themes. *Young Children, 46*(1), 24–29.

Overby, L.Y. (Ed.). (1991). *Early childhood creative arts.* Reston, VA: American Alliance for Health, Physical Education, Recreation and Dance.

Poest, C.A., Williams, J.R., Witt, D.D., & Atwood, M.E. (1990). Challenge me to move: Large muscle development in young children. *Young Children, 45*(5), 4–10.

Raines, S.C., & Canady, R.J.(1989 and 1991). *Story S-t-r-e-t-c-h-e-r-s: Activities to Expand Children's Favorite Books* and *More Story S-t-r-e-t-c-h-e-r-s.* Mt. Rainier, MD: Gryphon House.

Rivkin, M. (Ed.). (1992). Science is a way of life. *Young Children, 47*(4), 4–8.

Strickland, D.S., & Morrow, L.M. (Eds.). (1989). *Emerging literacy: Young children learn to read and write.* Newark, DE: International Reading Association.

Sullivan, M. (1982). *Feeling strong, feeling free: Movement exploration for young children.* Washington, DC: NAEYC.

Williams, R.A., R.D. Rockwell, & E.A. Sherwood. (1983). *Hug a tree and other things to do outdoors with young children.* Mt. Rainer, MD: Gryphon House.

Workman, S., & Anziano, M.C. (1993). Curriculum webs: Weaving connections from children to teachers. *Young Children, 48*(2), 4–9.

Being with children and creating a joyful, inclusive classroom atmosphere

Catron, C. (1976). Circles of sunshine. *Young Children, 31*(6), 449–459.

Curry, N.E., & Johnson, C.N. (1990). *Beyond self-esteem: Developing a genuine sense of human value.* Washington, DC: NAEYC.

Greenberg, P. (1986). Ideas that work with young children. The take-a-minute teacher. *Young Children, 42*(1), 21–22.

Greenberg, P. (1988). Ideas that work with young children. Positive self-image: More than mirrors. *Young Children, 43*(4), 57–59.

Greenberg, P. (1988). Ideas that work with young children. The difficult child. *Young Children, 43*(5), 60–68.

Greenberg, P. (1992a). Ideas that work with young children. How to institute some simple democratic practices pertaining to respect, rights, roots, and responsibilities in any classroom (without losing your leadership position). *Young Children, 47*(5), 10–17.

Greenberg, P. (1992b). Teaching about Native Americans? Or teaching about people, including Native Americans? *Young Children, 47*(6), 27–30, 79–81.

Hitz, R., & Driscoll, A. (1988). Praise or encouragement? New insights into praise: Implications for early childhood teachers. *Young Children, 43*(5), 6–13.

Humphrey, S. (1989). Becoming a better kindergarten teacher: The case of myself. *Young Children, 45*(1), 16–22.

McCracken, J.B. (Ed.). (1986). *Reducing stress in young children's lives*. Washington, DC: NAEYC.

McCracken, J.B. (Ed.). (1990). *Helping children love themselves and others: A professional handbook for family day care*. Washington, DC: Children's Foundation.

Marshall, H.H. (1989). Research in review. The development of self-concept. *Young Children, 44*(5), 44–49.

Read, K. (1987). *Early childhood programs:Human relationships and learning* (8th ed.). New York: Holt, Rinehart.

Saracho, O.N., & Spodek, B. (1983). *Understanding the multicultural experience in early childhood education*. Washington, DC: NAEYC.

Stimson, E. (1988). Food for thought. Don't just say no to a child wanting attention when you're busy. *Young Children, 43*(5), 30–31.

Zavitovsky, D., Baker, K.R., Berlfein, J.R., & Almy, M. (1986). *Listen to the children*. Washington, DC: NAEYC.

Information About NAEYC

NAEYC is ...

. . . a membership-supported organization of people committed to fostering the growth and development of children from birth through age eight. Membership is open to all who share a desire to serve and act on behalf of the needs and rights of young children.

NAEYC provides ...

. . . educational services and resources to adults who work with and for children, including

- *Young Children,* the journal for early childhood educators
- **Books, posters, brochures,** and **videos** to expand your knowledge and commitment to young children, with topics including infants, curriculum, research, discipline, teacher education, and parent involvement
- An **Annual Conference** that brings people from all over the country to share their expertise and advocate on behalf of children and families

- **Week of the Young Child** celebrations sponsored by NAEYC Affiliate Groups across the nation to call public attention to the needs and rights of children and families
- **Insurance plans** for individuals and programs
- **Public affairs** information for knowledgeable advocacy efforts at all levels of government and through the media
- The **National Academy of Early Childhood Programs,** a voluntary accreditation system for high-quality programs for children
- The **National Institute for Early Childhood Professional Development,** providing resources and services to improve professional preparation and development of early childhood educators
- The **Information Service,** a centralized source of information sharing, distribution, and collaboration

For free information about membership, publications, or other NAEYC services ...

. . . call NAEYC at 202–232–8777 or 800–424–2460, or write to . . . NAEYC, 1509 16th Street, N.W., Washington, DC 20036–1426.